MW01173881

The COHESIVE COUPLE

Escape the Chaos. Connect Deeply. Build a Bigger Future—*Together*

by
Rebecca and James Lockwood
with Tom Bouwer

Printed in the United States of America

Published by Igniting Souls
PO Box 43, Powell, OH 43065
IgnitingSouls.com

LCCN: 2024920027
Paperback ISBN: 978-1-63680-404-0
Hardcover ISBN: 978-1-63680-405-7
e-book ISBN: 978-1-63680-406-4

Available in paperback, hardcover, e-book, and audiobook.

Any Internet addresses (websites, blogs, etc.) and telephone numbers printed in this book are offered as a resource. They are not intended in any way to be or imply an endorsement by Igniting Souls, nor does Igniting Souls vouch for the content of these sites and numbers for the life of this book.

Some names and identifying details may have been changed to protect the privacy of individuals.

The superscript symbol IP listed throughout this book is known as the unique certification mark created and owned by Instant IP™. Its use signifies that the corresponding expression (words, phrases, chart, graph, etc.) has been protected by Instant IP™ via smart contract. Instant IP™ is designed with the patented smart contract solution (US Patent: 11,928,748), which creates an immutable time-stamped first layer and fast layer identifying the moment in time an idea is filed on the blockchain. This solution can be used in defending intellectual property protection. Infringing upon the respective intellectual property, i.e., IP, is subject to and punishable in a court of law.

Text design and composition by Lauren Lane
Illustrations by Lauren Lane
Editing by Joyce Breeding and Bobby Langley

Table of Contents

Table of Contents
(continued)

Foreword
by Kary Oberbrunner

When I first heard the phrase "An Operating System for Couples," I knew they were onto something. Great companies run on an operating system; why not couples? It made perfect sense. Relationships, like businesses, thrive when there is clarity, direction, alignment, and intentionality. Without these elements, couples can easily become overwhelmed by day-to-day demands and the chaos of everyday life. This book offers a blueprint for creating an uncommon partnership where both individuals are aligned, working toward shared goals and connecting deeply.

What makes this book so practical and transformative? It takes the best tools and teachings from business thought-leaders, elite life coaches, and successful couples and shows other couples how to apply them to their relationship— creating an aligned vision, setting priorities, resolving conflicts, and achieving more than they ever thought possible—together. All in a simple system.

What stands out about this book is its emphasis on practical tools that you can make your own—in fact, the authors encourage you to make this system your own. Whether it's creating an aligned vision for the future, accomplishing bucket list items, or just staying in sync, The Cohesive Couple offers clear, actionable methods that can be personalized to meet the specific dynamics of any couple. It's this flexibility and adaptability that make the system so effective. No matter how long you've been together or what challenges you're facing, you'll find tools here that feel relevant and easy to implement, helping you build a stronger, more aligned partnership.

In my own work helping people unlock their potential, I've seen how crucial it is to use a framework or operating system, whether in business or personal life. I'm excited to endorse this book because it offers couples a clear path to building and maintaining a thriving partnership. These types of partnerships can change a relationship. Add up enough of these relationships, and you can change a community, a nation, and perhaps even the world. Presumptuous? You be the judge. Read the book, apply the principles, and you may just agree.

If you're looking to become an unstoppable team or to strengthen what you already have, this book provides the tools, strategies, and mindsets you need to create a deeply connected, successful relationship.

— Dr. Kary Oberbrunner, *Wall Street Journal* and *USA Today* Bestselling Author

Authors' Note

This isn't a couple's therapy book. If you're looking for that—you're in the wrong place. This book is for couples who want to build a bigger, bolder future together.

We wrote this book to give you, an ambitious couple that knows there can be more to life, a simple model to help you connect at a deeper level, create your best relationship and become unstoppable.

We're not PhDs armed with theoretical knowledge; instead, we are just people who learned a lot from practical experience, research, a desire to grow, trial and error and yes—some painful mistakes.

Throughout our journey, we've drawn insights from business tools and practices as well as strategies from life, marriage and performance coaches.

The result is a proven model that gives you practical tools to strengthen all aspects of your life and relationship. Each chapter could be a 5,000-page book, but we've kept it short and straightforward—as clear and concise as possible. Know that we intentionally left out many nuances and variations; this is not intended to be an academic read.

It doesn't matter what season of life you are in. You could be newly married or married for 40+ years. You could be in a second marriage. You could be 15 years in with 3 kids or have no kids. You could be financially stable or constantly worried about money. No matter where you are in life, our model and tools apply to you.

If you are a growth-mindset couple who understands that a cohesive team can be unstoppable—then this is your practical guide on how to do precisely that.

CHAPTER 1

How Did It Start?

"How did we even get here?"

Nothing seemed to be working the way we felt it should. We both felt lonely, overwhelmed, and disconnected. We realized we were going down the same river—in 2 different canoes. We knew we had to do something.

For us, life had taken over. With 2 small kids, a growing business, family commitments, friends, and everyday chaos, it just wasn't working. Sure, we still loved each other and had a good life from the outside, but our life and marriage didn't feel fulfilling.

We have an unconventional household by trad-itional definitions; I (Rebecca) run a thriving coaching practice, and James is a stay-at-home dad. I was growing with big goals but felt stuck—like I was the only one growing. I wanted to give up and start over. James wanted to bury his head in the sand; he couldn't dream or envision the future because he was simply trying to get through each day.

As James put it, "It all felt so overwhelming and intimidating to talk about the stuff that really mattered and to acknowledge how far apart we had drifted. I knew there was something better—that we should be in the same canoe, supporting each other, but I just didn't know how. Honestly, I was just trying to keep my head above water."

We were:

- Living unfulfilled
- Lacking alignment
- Letting problems divide us
- Swamped by conflicting priorities
- Feeling held back
- Poorly managing marriage, kids, work, and life
- Just plain unhappy

This might sound familiar and that is okay—well, not really. What I learned is that a lot of couples find themselves in exactly the same spot. Some chose to live with it. Some chose to end things. Some chose to take action.

I saw my client companies doing great things with the tools I was teaching them—increasing communication, building strong teams, achieving big goals... So I thought, if these things work for a company, why can't they work for my life and my relationship?

At first, James thought I was crazy as I pieced together tools and suggested weekly meetings, but once he began seeing results, he started to embrace it and really leaned in. "We tried a lot of things—a lot—until we started figuring it all out," adds James.

Are we perfect? Not even close. Do we have it all figured out all the time? Nope. It wasn't all smooth or easy. There were tears, tension and pain—and sometimes, it was downright funny.

The Cohesive Model[IP]

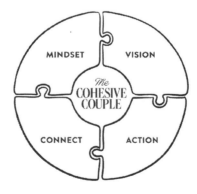

Today, we feel unstoppable. We are more in love, more connected, and living with more intention than ever before. During this journey, we came up with The Cohesive Model[IP]. By following this model, system and tools, we have achieved more than we thought possible.

Here are a few things we have checked off our list over the past few years (while running a company and daily family life):

✓ Spent 18 months on the road as a family, visiting 32 states and 43 national parks

✓ Spent 4 consecutive winter ski seasons in Colorado

✓ Increased net worth by 300%

✓ Have a team in place to support our life so we can stop doing things that drain our energy

✓ Achieved many bucket list items including James and our 12-year-old son Lucas going to Everest base camp

✓ Consistently hitting health and longevity targets

✓ Written a book to share our passion with the world (hint: you're reading it!)

Here's the thing: we aren't sitting on millions in the bank or blessed with unlimited resources. In fact, we're just like you—navigating life's ups and downs, striving to make the most of ourselves, our relationship and our family. Our accomplishments are the result of getting aligned, deepening our connection, improving our communication, working together and consistently following the model.

In essence, we created a model that empowers us to navigate our future together. It feels like we are back in the same canoe, supporting each other, paddling in sync and moving forward in unison. If one of us starts to fall out of the canoe, we help pull the other back in.

I learned one other amazing thing—the benefit of having a shared language. Now, we can tease out problems with more ease, solve problems more quickly, and laugh at our abundant quirks by having a shared language.

So why The 'Cohesive' Couple? Various diction-aries define cohesive as: united and working together effectively or of forming a united whole. A definition I love is: the state of sticking togeth-er, being in close agreement and working well together. I can't think of a better way to describe a thriving marriage or partnership.

Ultimately, *The Cohesive Couple* is about provid-ing a framework or process for aligning and prior-itizing what truly matters to you both. It is about knowing you both decided to live your best life to-gether, making the most of your time, talents, and opportunities. It is about saying no to the unim-portant so you can say yes to the important, for you, as a team.

By reading this book, you are embarking on your Cohesive Journey. We'll first explain The Cohesive Model and how it works. Then, we'll explain the Elements that form the foundation for The Cohesive Couple.

Finally, we'll conclude with an ongoing plan to keep you on track and help you actualize your dreams.

CHAPTER 2

Why Do We Need This?

"There was a light bulb moment – I already ran my business with tools and a model, but it never occurred to me how to apply it to my personal life."

L et's start by understanding what a model is. Every couple has one, whether they know it or not. It is how they set priorities, divide tasks, parent, use resources, dream, set goals, support each other, solve problems, approach the world, view their mind, body, and soul, communicate and connect. It is their system of subconscious values and behaviors.

However, most couples never think about their relationship or life through this lens. The consequence is mediocrity—just floating through life, or worse, chaos, frustration and/or divorce. Ultimately, without following a deliberate model, they never realize their full potential as individuals, a couple or as a family.

Need some stats?

- 50% is the approximate divorce rate in the US
- 40% of Americans are pessimistic about the institution of marriage
- 25% stay married because they are worried about what other people will say if they get divorced
- 47% of couples report staying together because of kids

That sounds pretty awful. What if these couples had a model or framework with tools to connect, communicate, set goals, resolve issues—and stay in the same canoe? Imagine the relationships that could have been turned from survivable or average into awesome.

This is precisely why a model is important. You may be thinking, "This sounds like it will kill all spontaneity and romance. This doesn't sound fun at all." And you'd be dead wrong.

Our research, supported by the works of David H. Olsen and 1,200 other studies over the past 30 years, demonstrates that achievement is at its peak when couples maintain a moderate amount of structure combined with a high degree of alignment[IP].

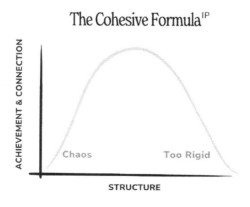

The Cohesive Formula[IP]

Too little structure and chaos ensues. Too much structure and life becomes rigid, inflexible or code-pendent. Our system gives you the framework to create just enough structure to become unstoppable.

In truth, a couple using a system will realize more of their dreams and ambitions. They will experience greater happiness, have more fun, live longer, embrace spontaneity, nurture heightened romance and intimacy, overcome life's challenges through mutual support and connect at an extremely intimate level.

If that sounds like something you want, here are a few more things you should know:

- This is not therapy and this is not rigid
- This is yours to use and adapt to make it work for you
- This is about your future always being brighter than your past

You can take the tools, concepts and approaches as suggestions and customize them to make them yours. The model takes proven business, life, and marriage coaching tools and adapts them to work for couples and their relationships.

> *"You do not rise to the level of your goals.*
> *You fall to the level of your systems."*
> – JAMES CLEAR, *ATOMIC HABITS*

"We're sharing what worked for us because we've already seen the incredible impact it can have on others," said James. "We fully expect people to change it and figure out what works best for them. In fact, a huge benefit for any couple is just starting the discussions our model will initiate."

CHAPTER 3

How Does It Work?

THE COHESIVE MODEL

"This model gave us the alignment to encourage our dreams, space to connect, and put a structure on how to get there."

Now that you know why a model is important and what it can do for you, it is important to understand The Cohesive Model and how it works.

Every extraordinary couple is rock solid in 4 Elements: Mindset, Connect, Vision, and Action[IP]. Think of these Elements like pieces of a jigsaw puzzle. Just as a puzzle remains unfinished without each piece, your relationship's picture remains incomplete without these critical Elements.

The Cohesive Model™

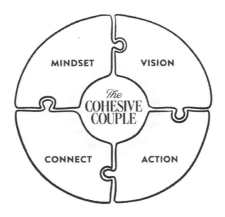

To start, we'll give you a high-level view of why each Element is critical and how to strengthen each one.

The Mindset Element

Let's face it. Without the right mindset, nothing else is possible: not deep connection, not great communication, not improved understanding of each other, not achievement of dreams, not alignment on vision and not action. That's why we start with mindset and the most important part of Mindset – Awareness and Curiosity.

Do you know anyone who thinks nothing is possible? Perhaps someone with a victim mentality, always blaming others for every setback, or someone who finds problems in everything and then points fingers? Do you know anyone who gives up when they only have 1% left to finish? Imagine what a relationship would look like if such thinking prevailed. Surprisingly, many relationships suffer from this exact issue: unhealthy mindsets.

In such a relationship, limitations would be placed on everything. Nothing would be possible. Joy and celebration would be non-existent. Arguments would be endless. Dreams, goals, forward movement, and a deep, wonderful connection would be seemingly impossible.

Your mindset and awareness of it determine how you handle challenges, plan, achieve dreams, build a deep, lasting relationship, laugh, celebrate, support each other no matter what and create an intimate connection.

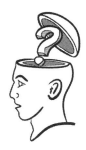

Imagine if Nelson Mandela had given up after 27 years in prison or if Beethoven had stopped composing because he was going deaf. Consider the resilience of Marie Curie, Stephen Hawking and even yourself.

These individuals, including you, are all examples of resilience—they did not let their circumstances shape their mindset. Instead, they used their mindset to shape their circumstances. You can do the same with a strong and healthy mindset.

> *"What if life was not happening to you,*
> *it was happening for you."*
> – TONY ROBBINS, LIFE COACH

Now, imagine a relationship in which anything is possible fueled by a healthy, positive mindset. A place where there is a mutually beneficial solution to every challenge, where support is unconditional, and even arguments are viewed as positive events. It is a place where you both feel intimately in sync and every goal and dream is met. A place where anything is possible.

This is what being 100% in the Mindset Element looks like. You'll use several tools and approaches to increase your level of awareness and curiosity and cultivate a strong and healthy mindset. These tools, such as Clarity Time and Take The (Head) Trash Out, will be detailed in Chapter 4: Mindset.

The Connect Element

Do you ever feel lonely or disconnected from your partner? Maybe sometimes you feel misunderstood. At times, you might even wonder why you and your partner are arguing. Do you feel like Rebecca and James — on the same river but in 2 different canoes? Perhaps not even on the same river?

If so, the problem is a lack of Connection. You know when it's off, but it is hard to know how to fix it—even where to start.

> *"Connecting is not magic. Like any other skill, it can be learned, practiced and mastered."*
> – DR. JOHN GOTTMAN

"I always longed for a deep, meaningful connection but didn't know how to ask for it. It was so vague. I didn't know how to define it," stated Rebecca. "James felt like he was in an interrogation room when I approached it. It made him shut down. Worse, I didn't have any tools. I really felt helpless."

A poor connection often stems from a lack of intentionality, repetition, practice and understanding. In simpler terms, it's about not actively prioritizing your relationship with the appropriate tools and time.

Imagine not feeling like roommates but like soul mates. Both of you feel seen, heard and aligned.

You have date nights and rituals that keep you connected. You spend quality time together, not just a lot of time. You can actually talk about your level of connection.

You share an unequaled level of trust and vulnerability. You can talk about and tell each other everything and anything. You approach the world as 'we'. You become the couple that people look at and say, "Look at them. They are truly connected." That is being 100% in the Connect Element.

You'll use several tools and approaches to increase your level of awareness and to cultivate a strong, healthy connection. These tools, such as Bucket List, Kolbe A™ to A, Shared Language and Cohesive Rituals, will be detailed in Chapter 5: Connect.

The Vision Element

Have you ever thought you agreed on long-term plans only to find out later that you really didn't? Have you ever talked about dreams that never materialized? Have you ever argued about dreams that seemed to be in conflict with each other? If so, you're not alone; this is a common challenge faced by many couples.

James wanted a house with a white picket fence, while Rebecca wanted to be a nomad, RVing around America. "We kept going in circles, which turned into arguments, pushing us further apart," said Rebecca. "It was very frustrating for both of us."

A misaligned vision is a common problem caused by a lack of clarity, agreement and documentation. You might have similar goals but different ideas on how to reach them. Alternatively, you might have goals that seem conflicting. How can you both possibly get what you want?

Now, imagine yourselves with a written vision of your future. You've figured out how both of you can achieve your individual and joint goals—together. You've agreed on it. You've prioritized it. You've written it down.

You've decided how you'll work on it together. Everything is in sync. When life gets in the way, you're able to stay focused and work through it together. You'll also be aligned on what to say NO to.

"When we boiled it down, we realized we could have both—we didn't have to compromise. It was incredibly liberating, and the problems stopped coming between us; instead, they became problems to solve together—they were even kind of fun to solve," continued Rebecca.

"Now we have a home in Ohio as our base and we spend at least 5 months traveling to new places and skiing in the winter. Even better, we've put a stop to the endless arguments and discussions and are making real progress."

This is what being 100% in the Vision Element looks like. You'll both be working together towards the same long-term and short-term goals. There will be less frustration and fewer arguments. More will get done in less time. You'll be able to say no to things that don't align with your vision.

The tool we developed to strengthen the Vision Element is called the Cohesive Vision & Plan[IP], or "CVP[IP]." It helps you get aligned around the answers to 8 simple questions:
1. What are your Values?
2. What is your Why?
3. What is your Big Dream?
4. What are your Rituals?
5. What is your 3 Year Vision?
6. What are your 1 Year Goals?

7. What are your 90 Day Rocks?
8. What is your 1 Commitment to Me^{IP}?

Once you are aligned and have answered these 8 questions, you'll be on your way to being 100% rock solid in the Vision Element. This tool will be explained fully in Chapter 6.

The Action Element

So now, you have a vision around which you are aligned. You are approaching life with the right mindset. You are deepening and strengthening your connection. But what do you do to make it a reality? To make it stick?

Rebecca and James encountered that same dilemma. "We were putting our vision on paper, going to seminars, learning about ourselves, but when we'd get back home, life got busy and we just reverted to the way it used to be," said James.

"It was frustrating. We tried but we just didn't know how to keep it going. We didn't know how to take action or create lasting habits from all we had learned."

Imagine a couple with the best intentions but struggling to follow through. They schedule date nights but they rarely happen. Time is double booked with different activities. Kids' sports and schedules make them feel more like an Uber service.

Agreed-upon projects start (sometimes) but never reach completion—they both think the other person is going to do the next step—arguments ensue. Activities aren't assigned, agreed upon or led by the person who is best at doing them.

This is caused by a lack of focus, accountability, clarity and prioritization. These symptoms are the direct result of a lack of a systematic approach to getting things done—weekly, monthly, quarterly, and annually.

Now, picture a couple where 90% of date nights actually happen, weekly to-dos are checked off, progress towards their vision is crystal clear, they prioritize and make adjustments as needed, they have fun and they celebrate their success. They are in control and living their best life every day, week, month and year.

"We get a chance to check in with each other and sync our calendars – there are a lot fewer surprises. We also know who has committed to completing which tasks. It feels like we have a rhythm in our relationship," said James.

"By failing to prepare, you are preparing to fail."
– BENJAMIN FRANKLIN

This is what being 100% in the Action Element looks, sounds and feels like. You have a cadence and rhythm to life to stay focused, aligned and connected each week, month and quarter. You are accomplishing the things on your CVP (rituals, dreams, goals, etc.). You are making your future happen – together.

The tools to get you to 100% include Weekly Sync[IP], 7 Day Calendar Review, Pink Jobs & Blue Jobs[IP] and Money Sync[IP]. These tools will be detailed in Chapters 7 to 10.

Now you know why a Model is essential, how each Element of the Model can help you, and what you look like when each Element is 100% rock solid.

You and your partner will be aligned on your vision, approaching life with a strong and healthy mindset, connecting more deeply, communicating more effectively and easily, and getting results through intentional action.

Summary of the Cohesive Model

MINDSET

(Chapter 4)

Being aware of your thinking, approach to life and your relationship with a strong and healthy mindset

TOOLS

Awareness and Curiosity, Clarity Time, Take The 'Head' Trash Out

CONNECT

(Chapter 5)

Connecting more deeply through understanding, intentional actions and strengthening your 'we' muscle

TOOLS

Bucket List, Kolbe A™ to A, Shared Language, Cohesive Rituals

VISION

(Chapter 6)

Aligning on, agreeing on, and documenting who you are, what really matters and where you are going together

TOOLS

Cohesive Vision & Plan (CVP)

ACTION

(Chapter 7-10)

Getting results through focus, clarity, prioritization, accountability and a systematic approach

TOOLS

Sync Meetings, Calendar Review, Pink Jobs/Blue Jobs

If you'd like to get a baseline on your current state for each Element, we'd highly suggest you take the Relationship Check Up in Appendix A.

CHAPTER 4

Are You Aware of Your Mindset?

—— MINDSET TOOLS ——

"Your relationship will never grow beyond your level of thinking."

We understand that you might be eager to dive into the seemingly more tangible Elements of The Cohesive Couple like Connect, Vision, and Action. However, achieving connection, developing a shared aligned vision, and taking action, hinges on being aware of your Mindset (i.e. your thinking).

Your Mindset is simply your views, assumptions, and beliefs about yourself, the world and your circumstances. It creates your model of reality. It determines how you think and feel; it influences your choices and behaviors. As a result, it is a primary factor in the success of your relationships, your health and your life. Surprisingly, many of us underestimate the power and impact of a healthy Mindset.

The rest of this chapter can be summed up with 3 questions:

1. Do you reframe things in a positive way or a negative way?
2. Do you practice reframing things on a regular basis?
3. How would your relationship change if you reframed your Mindset?

Awareness and Curiosity

Yes, we all know we should have a 'good Mindset,' but how often do we seek to improve it or are even aware of our thinking? How often are we actively conscious of how our mindset is impacting our actions and choices? How often do we reframe our thinking? If our Mindset is the lens through which we view the world... How can we ensure that the lens isn't foggy or blurred?

To illustrate this, in one of our workshops Jeff said, "I used to assign meaning to a lot of things. Brittney would be in a bad mood and I always thought it was something I had done. It turns out that most of the time, she'd just had a rough day."

In short, living your best life requires an Awareness and a conscious understanding of your Mindset. Awareness requires Curiosity—a willingness to explore what you are thinking, why you are thinking that way, and how it impacts your actions.

Have you ever traveled to another country and had it change your thinking because of what you saw?

Danish parents frequently leave their sleeping babies in their strollers or prams outside of restaurants and coffee shops. They feel the cold makes for better sleep and allows parents hands-free time. Can you imagine parents from some other countries doing this?

When you are Curious, Awareness results in good decision-making even in the face of hard decisions. It helps you ask yourself important questions such as:

- Should I take the emotion out of this?
- Am I giving meaning to something that has no meaning?
- Am I overreacting?
- Do I need to think about this differently?
- Are my habits supporting my goals?
- Am I viewing this as an obligation or an opportunity?

With Curiosity and Awareness, you'll find it easier to set boundaries and communicate effectively with your partner. You'll find yourself less affected by the opinions and judgments of others. Correcting bad habits becomes easier; fear and stress are reduced.

A truly great Mindset creates better partners, parents, friends and leaders. You'll be great examples for each other. You'll be able to help each other when your Mindset slips into an unhealthy mode. Together, you will generate a positive tone in your relationship. And those are just some of the benefits of a healthy mental outlook.

For example, do you have to take the kids to school or do you have an opportunity to create a ritual and bond with them? Did my husband make the most awful coffee in the world or did he bring it to me out of love? Do I have to mow the yard, or do I have an opportunity to get exercise, fresh air and sun?

Your current thoughts and beliefs stem from your unique set of experiences, your background and your exposure to different perspectives. With Curiosity about how this impacts your Mindset, you can reframe your thoughts and beliefs about your internal and external worlds. How you reframe depends on your view of resources and possibilities about yourself and the world.

Abundance & Scarcity

Let's talk about Abundance and its evil twin, Scarcity; they describe how you view your internal and external worlds.

How do you view the amount of resources and opportunities in the world? Do you view yourself as worthy or unworthy? Can everyone realize their dreams or just a few brilliant people? Is the world full of opportunity, or are those opportunities limited? Have you put limitations on yourself, or do you live in a world of possibility?

Living in a world of Scarcity is rooted in a 'there is only so much and I need to get mine' mentality. People who think this way feel threatened by the success of others; they hoard resources, information, or opportunities out of fear.

They act from a place of anxiety or trepidation. They tell themselves they don't have enough, are not enough, or can't. What could Scarcity look like in your own life and relationship?

- I don't have enough time
- I can't have a great connection with my partner
- I don't have enough money
- I can't have enough intimacy
- I am stuck in my current situation
- I don't have enough to share
- I can't take risks or be vulnerable
- I don't believe I can learn, grow or change
- I'm not good enough

On the other hand, living in a world of Abundance reflects a belief that there is enough out there for everyone. An Abundance Mindset also reflects a positive view of your ability to grow and learn. Opportunities and possibilities are limitless.

People who think this way are happy when others succeed as they believe it takes nothing away from them. They seek to learn and improve. What does abundance look like?

- I can make enough time
- I can create a strong connection with my partner
- I can create enough money or find a way to make something happen
- I can develop great intimacy
- I can change and am in charge of my situation
- I believe sharing now pays dividends in the future
- I believe being vulnerable and taking risks creates growth, confidence and connection
- I believe in myself and my ability to learn and grow
- I am good enough

Finally, here are a few comparisons you can come back to when reframing your Mindset with Abundance thinking.

ABUNDANCE VS. SCARCITY THINKING [IP]

ABUNDANCE THINKING	SCARCITY THINKING
Optimistic	Pessimistic
Possible	Impossible
Worthy	Unworthy
Hopeful	Hopeless
Confident	Doubtful
Encouraging	Discouraging
Positive	Negative
Trusting	Suspicious
Adventurous	Cautious
Opportunity	Obligation

With Abundance and Scarcity in mind (pun intended), let's look at examples of how to reframe your internal and external worlds.

Reframing Your External World

Part of a great mindset (and living a great life) is the ability to see or reframe things happening in your external world differently (i.e., the availability of resources and opportunities). Are things happening 'to' you or 'for' you? What meaning are you giving things, and is it helping or hindering you?

It's easy to be a victim when you think about the external world. It's easy to think things are out of your control or unfair or 'just the way they are'.

But what if you asked yourself, is there something positive I can take from this experience? How can I change? Was there a lesson in it that I needed to learn? How can I reframe the situation in my head? What if I looked for the positive or opportunities in this situation?

So how can you apply this to your life? Let's take a look at a few examples with a reframe:

Have you ever seen a great athlete who threw a tantrum whenever a call didn't go their way? Perhaps they would blame everyone else for a loss? They seem to think they would have won if not for everyone else's mistakes or biases against them. After all, it is always someone else's fault, right?

These types of people derive a lot of their self-esteem and sense of self-worth from winning and being correct. They focus on proving their intelligence and/or talent and harbor a deep fear of failure. They view their external world from a Scarcity perspective.

What if they simply asked, "What if I had practiced more?" or "Is this a chance for me to demonstrate dignity, composure and professionalism?" or "What can I do to change the future?".

"Nothing in life has any meaning except the meaning you give to it. Will you give your past a meaning filled with hurt and pain, or will you realize that it's what made you who you are today?"
– TONY ROBBINS

When the pandemic hit and people had to work from home, James and Rebecca traveled around the USA with their kids. Other couples moved permanently to a vacation home or a better lifestyle location. Many couples looked for opportunities like this. Where can you reframe your external world with an Abundance Mindset?

Reframing Your Internal World

So that's your external world; what about your internal world? Your internal world is about how you view yourself and your capacity for development and improvement.

Have you ever heard Les Brown's story about being labeled as educable mentally retarded? Teachers didn't realize his true potential and he started to believe it – until one day a professor helped him reframe this, and he went on to become a wildly successful motivational speaker, political commentator and multi-term state representative in Ohio.

Where might this be happening to you? Do you believe that your abilities and talents are limited and can't be significantly changed? Or, do you believe you can learn or do almost anything?

Let's look at Michael Jordan, who was a truly great NBA player. In fact, when he joined the 'Dream Team' for the 1992 Barcelona Olympics, he was at the peak of his career. Despite being surrounded by other basketball superstars, he was one of the few players to ask the coaches to stay after practice and work with him to improve his game.

During his illustrious career, Michael Jordan missed ~9,000 shots, lost ~300 games and missed the winning shot 26 times. Yet with all these 'failures,' he is still considered one of the greatest NBA players of all time. He derived his value from improving, learning and taking on challenges. He never let himself get too comfortable with only being really, really good.

This is a real challenge in relationships. Things can get very comfortable, cozy, and easy, or perhaps just not bad enough to address. Don't accept mediocrity or 'good enough.' Adopt a mindset of always improving (while celebrating wins along the way) and embracing change, not avoiding it. After all, change is the only constant in life.

In relationships, extremely different views on Scarcity and Abundance result in very different approaches to your relationship, kids, chosen work, abilities, problem-solving and opportunities. Simply understanding each other's default view and discussing it is a great step forward.

Be...Do...Have...

Most people approach life using a Have...Do...Be... philosophy. They believe that once they Have something (e.g., money, time, love), then they can Do something (e.g., travel, start a business, engage in hobbies) that will allow them to Be a certain way (e.g., happy, content, fulfilled).

However, successful people go at this in the opposite order: Be...Do...Have. First, Be the person you aspire to be by embracing the right mindset and heightening your self-awareness. Then, Do the actions that align with that identity, including your habits and surrounding yourself with like-minded individuals. Finally, by BEING and DOING, you will HAVE what you want.

"I always thought that if I could just get that perfect, high-paying job, I could really do what I wanted and have happiness," said Sarah. "What I realized was that I would never have what I wanted (happiness) unless I changed internally first."

This highlights a key distinction between these 2 mindsets, their starting points. The Have… Do… Be… mindset places emphasis on external achievements and possessions. These are seen as the foundation for happiness.

The Be…Do…Have Mindset starts with your internal state. By improving your thinking and then aligning your actions with your values and goals, external achievements will naturally follow. This requires you to be unattached to outcomes and instead focus on your identity and what you must be committed to in order to embody that identity.

So how do you apply this to your relationship? If you want a better relationship, you have to embody the identity of someone who is committed to a great relationship. Relationships require work and commitment—committing to someone in a relationship is the easy part. It's the commitment to the commitment that is the work.

Don't measure short-term results; instead, measure short-term actions or commitments. This approach leads to a more fulfilling relationship where actions and achievements result from you just being you—and being happy with that—rather than chasing externally defined parameters. Ultimately, you create and Have the life you both want.

OK, so that's a lot of great information so far and hopefully you've become more Curious about how impactful reframing your mindset can be. But how do you practice this?

Here are 3 tools to help you exercise and improve your Mindset: Clarity Time, Take The (Head) Trash Out, and Progress Not Perfection. As you review these tools, refine and adjust them to make them work for you.

If you want to enhance your Mindset to improve your relationship, please commit to some variation of these. Your Mindset, like anything else, needs exercise.

Clarity Time[IP]

How often do you give yourself time to think? There's a reason why your best ideas often come to you while showering, hiking, or knitting. It is because your mind is free to wander and wonder. You're free to think.

Clarity Time involves setting time and space aside by yourself each week to just let yourself think. Sounds crazy, right? Honestly, how often have you said, "I just wish I had a few minutes to be by myself, think and reset?" Clarity Time is a tool to help and a great weekly habit to form.

Here's what you do:

- **Block Off Time on Your Calendar:** Do what works for you (30 to 120 minutes once a week).
- **Be Dogmatic:** Don't let anything interfere with your time. Don't reschedule. When it is on the calendar, keep that time sacred. Make it a habit.
- **No Distractions**: No electronics. No phone. No email. No nothing.
- **Take a Pen and a Piece of Paper:** Yup, no electronics.
- **No Agenda:** There might be things you want to think about and that's okay, but don't keep a formal agenda.
- **Be Amazed:** Imagine what comes out of your head and onto that piece of paper[IP].

It sounds simple, but it will take discipline to make it a habit. Don't like some of the ideas? At a minimum, please apply the concept; you'll benefit greatly from it.

Clarity Time [IP]

What IS Clarity Time	What is NOT Clarity Time
Time by yourself	Time with others
Coffee on your porch	Intense workouts
Tea in the woods on a log	Watching a movie
Sit on a park bench	Scrolling social media
Nature walks	Playing a video game
Long solo runs	Eating out
Journaling or meditation	Driving in traffic

Take The (Head) Trash Out [IP]

You have to admit, Head Trash is fun to say. It is also a powerful concept. Head Trash refers to the negative and limiting thoughts, beliefs, and mental narratives that get in your way.

Head Trash can be things like "I always screw that up," "They always do that," "They have it in for me," "They may be thinking bad things about me," or "She doesn't like me."

Here's the funny thing: most of the time you're the only one thinking about it; it is not taking up any of their mental space or energy. It is the story you are telling yourself.

Head Trash is your critical inner voice that undermines your confidence, distorts your perceptions of reality and gets in the way of your ability to achieve goals. These are your limiting beliefs. It can also really cause problems with your partner.

The tool we use to address Head Trash is called Take The (Head) Trash Out. Think of pulling all those limiting and negative thoughts and beliefs out of your head and throwing them in a trash bin. Next, picture yourself taking that trash bin to the curb and getting rid of it.

Being aware of your own Head Trash or asking your partner, "Is this my Head Trash?" can be an effective way to develop a healthy mindset. Clarity Time and Take The (Head) Trash Out will help you manage and mitigate your own Head Trash.

Progress Not Perfection

Finally, a healthy Mindset is focused on improvement. It is like learning how to ride a bike. In the initial stages of riding, there's a fair share of wobbling and falling. You might have been frustrated, but you didn't criticize yourself harshly. You didn't quit—you just kept trying with resilience and determination.

Improvement comes with time and effort. Making mistakes is part of the journey in life and with your partner. Couples with this mindset will laugh when things go sideways and say, "Yup, that didn't work out so well. What should we do differently next time to move forward?"

This should be a guiding principle for your life: don't let imperfection paralyze you. Aim for progress and learning, not perfection. Celebrate your progress, learn from mistakes, and move steadily toward your goals. Acknowledge the past, learn its lessons and move forward. You'll find many cases every day where you can apply 'Progress not Perfection.'

Summary Of Mindset

Mindset impacts everything we do. While no person is 100% in any Mindset 100% of the time, these approaches and tools will help you reframe your mindset about your life and in your relationship.

Awareness, Curiosity, and Abundance thinking will cultivate a healthy Mindset resulting in a deeper connection, a happier life, and achievement of your vision together.

Connect Tool	What It Does
CLARITY TIME	Provide space and time for a higher level of thinking without distractions
TAKE THE 'HEAD' TRASH OUT	Destroy your critical inner voice that undermines your confidence
PROGRESS NOT PERFECTION	Celebrate improvement and small wins to keep the momentum going

CHAPTER 5

Are We Really Connected?

— CONNECT TOOLS —

"I connected with my husband in a different way. It was like a big wake-up call for us to talk about things like our communication styles and Cohesive Rituals."

Connection. You've felt it. You know what it is. And yet it is elusive and hard to describe.

You've probably seen that couple sitting on a bench or holding hands while walking into the grocery store. They're laughing, touching and completely at ease with each other—they are in sync. You can tell that they not only love each other but that they are in love; that they have a deep, intimate connection.

On the flip side, you probably also know a couple that has been together for a while—they still love each other but that intense connection seems to have faded. They made it through their wedding day, honeymoon and a few years; however, the spark that once defined their relationship isn't as vibrant anymore.

Life made things complicated—that initial strong feeling of connection has slowly faded away and diminished. It has become a connection of relative safety and familiarity; to put it starkly, they are living as roommates.

The lack of a deep and intimate connection can lead couples to feel:

- Unfulfilled
- A lack of closeness and intimacy
- Not on the same page
- Out of control
- Crushed by conflicting priorities
- Poorly managing life (career, marriage, kids)
- More like roommates than partners

This happens when there's not enough focus, practice, purpose, and understanding of ourselves and our partner. Connection begins to fade when we can't, don't know how to, or won't deal with challenging and awkward problems—the hard conversations that can actually build connection. It will fade if you do not devote enough focused time to your connection.

This causes trust and vulnerability to decline, resulting in a vicious cycle where unconditional love, support and acceptance keep going down—until they disappear. The solution is simple (though not always easy).

Connection, like any muscle, needs constant exercise just to maintain its current state; it takes hard work and sometimes, even a little pain to help it grow. You just have to put in the time and effort.

*"One of the greatest gifts of a relationship
is the ability to see the world through the eyes of
another person, intimately, deeply, profoundly,
in a way we're almost never able to do with
another human being."*

– DR. JOHN GOTTMAN

It could be as simple as creating a small ritual. These are special moments you share, often known only to the 2 of you. They will strengthen your connection and enrich your Relationship Bank Account with emotional currency.

Relationship Bank Account

Similar to the way your money accumulates in your bank account, a Relationship Bank Account is the amount of goodwill, trust, positive feelings, and demonstrated supportive behaviors that build up in a relationship.

All the things you do either put 'money' in your relationship account or take 'money' out. They contribute to your connection or deplete it. Ask your-self, "Did I take from the account or give to the account today?"

For example, how often do you 'turn towards' your partner? When they point something out of the car window, make a small sigh, or reach for your hand, do you accept their request to connect or do you turn away?

Those are moments in which you can choose to add deposits to your Relationship Bank Account. You can choose to turn towards your partner in these moments, or you can choose to turn away.

The benefits of a positive Relationship Bank Account are self-evident: less conflict, greater trust, fewer misunderstandings, greater appreciation and a continuous deepening of your connection.

Like your monetary bank account, be conscious of this account. It takes 5 positive interactions to put $1 in and only 1 negative interaction to lose that same dollar. Right now, is your Relationship Bank Account overflowing or in debt?

Shared Language

An important ingredient in living by The Cohesive Model is the development and use of a Shared Language. While it might seem obvious, here are just a couple of benefits:

- It is **easier to understand each other** by helping you interpret expressions, desires, and concerns in the same way. It reduces the likelihood of misunderstandings.
- It **streamlines communication** as there is less need for explanations or clarifications. This is especially helpful in times of conflict or when making important decisions.
- **You get it** when the other person expresses love, appreciation or other emotions.
- It **facilitates conflict resolution** because you can more clearly understand the other's perspective which leads to more constructive solutions.

- It **enhances trust and security**. Clear communication builds trust.
- It **makes life more fun** by being able to tease each other about your styles and different personalities.

In essence, a Shared Language in a relationship acts as a foundational tool that promotes better understanding, emotional depth and more robust connections, helping you develop a healthier, more fulfilling partnership. Another tool we find helpful in furthering an understanding of how you both think, communicate and solve problems is the Kolbe A system.

Kolbe A to A Comparison

Your brain is naturally wired to solve challenges, situations or issues in a certain way. The Kolbe A system helps you see your natural tendencies—where you operate most comfortably when solving problems.

These instinctive approaches are categorized into 4 areas:

- *Fact Finder:* How much detail you need
- *Follow Through:* How likely you are to follow processes
- *Quick Start:* How comfortable you are with uncertainty and risk
- *Implementor:* How you touch or see things to get to solutions

So what happens when you put yours next to your partners? On the next page are Rebecca and James' Kolbe results put side by side.

You can visually see where conflict can occur (subtle hint: large differences in scores). Given that, what might this look like in a conversation? How might that cause a decrease in connection?

Kolbe A Results

REBECCA AND JAMES LOCKWOOD

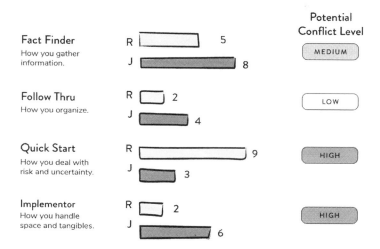

Here is a conversation you might be able to relate to.

> Rebecca: "I'd like to get away for a week and go camping."
>
> James: "Yeah, I love the idea."
>
> Rebecca: "Great."

The next evening:

> James: "Hey, how was your day?"
>
> Rebecca: "Awesome. I made reservations to go camping next week. Isn't that awesome? I didn't see anything critical on the calendar."
>
> James: "Huh? We didn't agree to that! What were you thinking?"

Rebecca is thinking: "We discussed, we agreed, what is your problem?"

James is thinking: "How could she do this? I've got to figure out the kids' schedules, school, dogs, pack, buy groceries and all these things. We haven't even talked about if this fits in our budget or agreed on when we want to do this."

This highlights how a seemingly simple conversation can go sideways, creating frustration and resentment. It certainly degraded their level of connection. Why?

Rebecca is a high Quick Start; James is a low Quick Start. Rebecca is a moderate Fact Finder; James is a high Fact Finder. With a bit more understanding of just these 2 differences, the conversation could have gone like this:

> Rebecca: "I'd like to get away for a week and go camping."
>
> James: "Yeah, I love the idea, but can we talk about specific plans tomorrow?"

Rebecca: "Great. Thanks for letting me know you'll need time to process this – how about if we talk about it on date night?"

James: "Thanks for not making plans immediately. It sounds great. I'll be able to think about all the things that we'll need to make this happen."

Now, Rebecca is thinking: "He heard that I want to do this, and we have a commitment to follow up and make it happen."

James is thinking: "She understands that I need a little time to process her ideas. I have some breathing room to see how we can do this together."

Simple? Yes. And you can see how understanding each other at this level can create better conversations and a stronger connection. It also highlights how you can support each other with different goals, needs and wants. You'll find your connection deepens with this type of awareness.

Love Languages®

Most likely you've heard of these or even read the book, *The Five Love Languages* by Gary Chapman. At its core, love languages are the ways you both express and experience love—including the relative importance you each place on those languages.

By knowing what makes your partner feel most loved and valued and by understanding the differences in how you demonstrate and interpret love, you will create a deeper and more meaningful connection. You both want to be seen, heard and valued.

Interestingly, many couples are speaking to and hearing each other in the wrong languages. They are not asking, "Am I expressing my love for you in a way that you truly value, appreciate and understand?"

Here is our take on it:

For example, one of Sue's primary Love Languages is Acts of Service; Bob's is Physical Touch. One night, Sue spends a lot of time preparing a nice meal for Bob, expressing her feelings through her Acts of Service lens.

When Bob just says "Thanks" and pulls out his phone to check messages, she feels unappreciated and disheartened and her face shows it. Bob is left wondering why she is suddenly in a bad mood.

Could this have gone differently? Very easily. Understanding Sue's Love Language, Bob could have put away his phone and said, "Wow, this looks amazing. I really appreciate the time this must have taken." If Sue understood Bob's Love Language, she could have pulled her chair closer, put her hand on his leg and winked.

It's the simple adjustments, the minor changes and a bit more awareness and attention that can significantly impact your connection.

Just like Mindset, Connect can seem like great information but many people struggle with how to put it into practice. Aside from using your knowledge in daily conversations with your partner, here are a couple of additional actions to take that can really deepen your connection.

Date Nights

When was the last time you went on an actual date? Was it fun and exciting like when you first started dating? Were you curious and asking each other lots of questions?

Unfortunately, dating for many couples has become a lost art. Life takes over or you get caught up in routines. But Date Nights are a critical part of connection and in some cases necessary to get to know your spouse again.

Here are a few reasons to have Date Nights:

- Enhance intimacy and romance
- Create powerful connection moments
- Create memories and rituals
- Add to your Relationship Bank Account
- Break monotony and reduce stress
- Deepen your connection
- Fulfill your (plural) Love Languages
- Demonstrate commitment

Let's face it: life is complex with kids, work, accidents, dogs getting into your garbage, etc. You need a Date Night just to break the cycle of everyday life. You also need one to remind yourselves of who you were before all those distractions.

Date Nights should be able to create a space to connect, have fun, laugh, etc. Here are some fun Date Night examples (BTW, it doesn't have to be at night):

- Breakfast for just the 2 of you (i.e., not with kids, friends or at a place where you'll see people you know.
- Symphony or concert
- Gun range
- Making a clay pot

- Take a cooking class
- Walk the dog
- Volunteer together
- Hike, kayak, swim, bike
- Picnic in backyard
- Recreate a past date
- Movie and Pajama Day
- Visit a museum
- Play a game (board or otherwise)

You get the idea. Date Nights can be simple and inexpensive. It doesn't need to be "fancy"—coffee in the living room or a walk around the block is just fine. They just need to be the 2 of you, no distractions, focused on each other and fun. Someone should own it and schedule it because if it doesn't get scheduled, it won't happen.

Do's

IP

Have fun. Laugh. Relax. Create space to connect. Talk about your vision or long term schedule. Talk about nothing. Have 1 owner (each week, month, or quarter). Be curious with each other. Ask lots of questions. Get a babysitter or somehow keep rug rats occupied. Avoid distractions. Get creative.

Don'ts

IP

Think it has to cost a lot of money. Talk about work, kids or logistics. Pick something where you will be easily distracted. Expect your partner to plan it. Feel the pressure to make it amazing. Make it your Weekly Sync meeting (more on this later). Take your 'other' woman/man with you (yes – your phone).

Bucket List

A Bucket List is all of the experiences, goals or achievements that you want to accomplish before you 'kick the bucket' which is a nice way of saying, die. It is fun to dream and discuss together – this could even be a great Date Night activity. Working together to create and then accomplish items on your Bucket List is an important element of Connect.

The items on the list can range from the more easily attainable (go to every ballpark in America) to ambitious dreams (live on Mars). They can also be very serious pursuits (run for public office) or very light-hearted wishes (meet a circus clown). Little or large, they are things you dream of doing.

Your Bucket List can be a blast to create together and a lot of fun to keep updated as you complete items. Here are some ideas to get you started:

- Ride a Zamboni
- Learn a new language
- Travel to every continent
- Do a TEDx talk
- Sing in front of a large audience
- Walk daughter down the aisle
- See Northern Lights
- Summit Mt. Denali
- Teach at local high school
- Complete Appalachian Trail
- Write a book (or 5)
- Go on an African Safari
- Stay in an island bungalow

- See All Blacks play
- Visit the Pyramids
- Serve on a not-for-profit board
- Visit Antarctica
- Learn to play the piano
- Fly a plane
- Kite Surf
- Learn Italian
- Learn to tie flies
- Go to an Opera
- Spend a week at a dude ranch

It is perfectly okay to have separate Bucket Lists and one shared list. One of you might like to go to an ice hotel in Norway; the other might think that is crazy. Maintaining individual lists will help you understand and support each other while simultaneously working towards shared dreams. Think of it like the picture on the next page.

For instance, James had Everest Base Camp on his list for years, and in their last Annual Sync Meeting (more on this later), Rebecca suggested he actually do it or take it off the list. Needless to say, the next year, all of Rebecca's airline miles went to help make that happen. This is an excellent example of helping each other, holding the other person accountable and pushing each other.

When you create a combined and an individual Bucket List, you are sharing your goals and dreams with each other. This will help you better understand and support your partner's desires and dreams. In turn, this fosters empathy and emotional closeness improving connection and a stronger sense of 'we.'

Working on your Bucket List requires encouragement and support, sometimes even pushing each other out of your comfort zones to try new things. It also builds trust and adds to your Relationship Bank Account.

The excitement and sense of adventure that many Bucket List items can generate help break the monotony of daily life. It keeps the spark in your relationship alive. They can be fun, challenging, exciting or even silly. They all accomplish the same thing: a strengthened connection.

When you achieve them, you create lasting memories and powerful moments that deepen your connection to each other. It also gives you another reason to celebrate success on your shared journey through life.

Cohesive Rituals[IP]

Cohesive Rituals will be detailed in the Vision chapter of the book. However, acting on them, establishing them and maintaining them is critical to the strength of your connection. Why?

"It's the small things done often that make the difference."

– DR. JOHN GOTTMAN

What is a Cohesive Ritual? Just a simple action that says, "I'm thinking about you" or "I love you." A good morning text, going to the same restaurant every Tuesday, bringing your partner a coffee every morning and buying a cannoli every time you pass your favorite bakery are all examples of Rituals.

Rituals create shared experiences and deepen trust; they strengthen and reinforce your values. Here are additional benefits they offer:

- Strengthen bonding
- Create shared memories
- Provide stability
- Foster emotional intimacy
- Cultivate appreciation
- Reinforce commitment
- Create a sense of belonging
- Mitigate stress
- Introduce fun and novelty
- Promote communication
- Celebrate milestones
- Establish your identity as a couple

In essence, Rituals are more than just routines; they are meaningful practices that strengthen the bond between partners. They provide structure, enrich the couple's emotional connection, foster a sense of belonging and identity, and serve as a foundation for building a resilient and enduring relationship. Through Rituals, couples can navigate life's challenges together, celebrate their love, and deepen their connection in meaningful ways.

Summary Of Connect

Connecting, like any muscle, needs constant exercise that adds to your Relationship Bank Account. As you develop a Shared Language, effective communication strengthens, issue solving becomes easier, and connection grows.

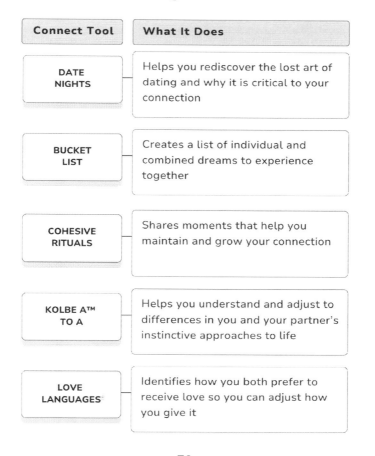

Connect Tool	What It Does
DATE NIGHTS	Helps you rediscover the lost art of dating and why it is critical to your connection
BUCKET LIST	Creates a list of individual and combined dreams to experience together
COHESIVE RITUALS	Shares moments that help you maintain and grow your connection
KOLBE A™ TO A	Helps you understand and adjust to differences in you and your partner's instinctive approaches to life
LOVE LANGUAGES	Identifies how you both prefer to receive love so you can adjust how you give it

CHAPTER 6

Is Our Vision Aligned and Written Down?

COHESIVE VISION & PLAN

"It was a chance for my husband and I to have conversations about our future dreams and not just tactics."

Have you ever tried to hike in a dense forest without a trail map to follow, wandering, unsure if each step brings you closer to the end or deeper into the maze? If so, you probably wished you had one.

Successful couples have a map. They have a crystallized and agreed-upon vision for the future—a set of future goals and dreams that is written down and regularly reviewed. This Vision clearly defines who you are, where you are going and how you will get there.

Sure, most couples talk about future plans and even their dreams, but many times, despite best intentions, they never materialize. Why? They are not written down and as a result, just stay as ideas and dreams for the future.

While not having them written down is a problem, an even bigger one is when both partners think they agree and in reality, don't. Or, even worse, disagree and can't find a solution or give up and avoid talking about it.

The tool that helps you define, agree on and write down your vision is called the Cohesive Vision & Plan[IP] or CVP[IP].

The CVP helps you both get your goals out of your heads and put down on paper. It gets you aligned with each other. Then, you can see where you are going together and start moving in the same direction – placing all your combined talents, energy, and unique abilities toward your goals. It will help you determine what's

important and what success, as you've defined it as a couple, will look like going forward.

By using the CVP, you will achieve your dreams as
a united couple. You will accomplish more in less
time than you ever thought possible. And you will
have fun doing it together. There are 8 questions
that make up the CVP[IP]:

1. What are your Values?
2. What is your Why?
3. What is your Big Dream?
4. What are your Cohesive Rituals?
5. What is your 3 Year Vision?
6. What are your 1 Year Goals?
7. What are your 90 Day Rocks?
8. What is your 1 Commitment to Me (C2Me[IP])?

The CVP is illustrated on the next page.

Cohesive Vision Plan[IP]

VALUES

BIG DREAM

WHY

COHESIVE RITUALS

3 YEAR VISION
Date: Dec 31, 20XX
Key Numbers:
- Income:
- Net Worth:
- Measurables:

1 YEAR GOALS
Date: Dec 31, 20XX
Key Numbers:
- Income:
- Net Worth:
- Measurables:

90 DAY ROCKS
Date: Mar 31, 20XX
Key Numbers:
- Income:
- Net Worth:
- Measurables:

COMMITMENT 2 ME

PARTNER 1

PARTNER 2

As you start to look into the future and answer these questions, it is important not to get stuck in the 'how' debate. That is, how will we ever get that done? Trust us on this. Have fun dreaming and you will find that most of your dreams will materialize. We'll show you the 'how' in later sections of this book.

Also, keep in mind that completing your CVP is a powerful connection tool. Have fun, laugh. Don't think you have to perfect it in one go. Spend 20% of the time to get it 80% right. Take it in little chunks so it doesn't start to feel overwhelming.

Now, we'll briefly explain why each section of the CVP is important and how each will help you maintain alignment and surpass your goals.

1. Values

Your Values are a set of fundamental beliefs and/or attributes that shape your identity as a couple. You can also think of them as mindsets if that helps. Typically there are just a few: 3 to 5 is recommended.

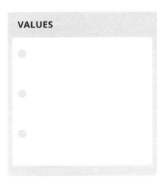

Values define who you are. As such, they will define your priorities, path and choices. It truly does all start with Values. They define your fundamental beliefs.

Here is an example of Rebecca and James' Values:
- Love, Listen, Be Present
- Take Responsibility
- 100% Possible
- Healthy Mind, Body and Soul

Note: Layla, the Lockwood's daughter, is an expert at calling her parents out when they don't exhibit their core values.

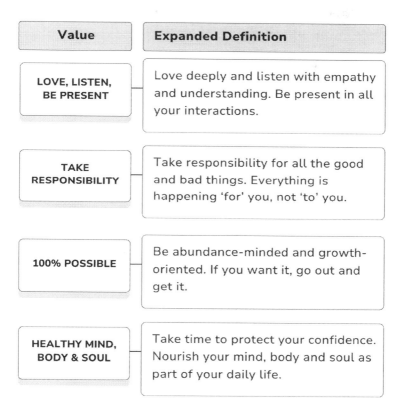

Value	Expanded Definition
LOVE, LISTEN, BE PRESENT	Love deeply and listen with empathy and understanding. Be present in all your interactions.
TAKE RESPONSIBILITY	Take responsibility for all the good and bad things. Everything is happening 'for' you, not 'to' you.
100% POSSIBLE	Be abundance-minded and growth-oriented. If you want it, go out and get it.
HEALTHY MIND, BODY & SOUL	Take time to protect your confidence. Nourish your mind, body and soul as part of your daily life.

These Values are expanded upon to include definitions of what they mean. This not only creates clarity but also establishes a clear understanding of the behaviors expected from each other.

Let's take 1 of those values: 'Love, Listen, Be Present,' and expand to a situation. Every time Rebecca and James have dinner, they leave their phones in another room to avoid the temptation of getting distracted and to ensure they are 100% present.

The expanded definition will help you 'walk the talk' and give you the ability to hold each other to an agreed-upon standard of behavior. After all, your behaviors demonstrate your priorities and Values.

> *"What you do speaks so loudly that I cannot hear what you say."*
> – RALPH WALDO EMERSON

You'll find that when you both are aligned around the same documented Values, life is easier and more harmonious. You might even find your Values determine who you select as friends and how you spend your time. They really are the cornerstone of everything you do and everything you aspire to be.

2. Why

While Values define who you are, your Why artic-ulates the purpose for your existence as a couple.

In other words, what is your shared purpose in life? To identify your Why, you'll be asking yourselves questions such as:

- What legacy are we leaving?
- What impact do we want to make in the world?
- What would we be proud of?
- What do we want to be remembered for?
- Why are we together?

This might sound really deep or hard but it can actually be fun—and it is definitely very powerful.

It is very easy to get distracted by all the craziness in the world: jobs, careers, housework, yardwork, conflicting schedules, email, texts, family demands, social events, church activities, etc. The list seems endless, filled with seemingly important and urgent matters. However, in reality, they may not be as significant as they first appear.

They may not align with your Values or your Why, and as a result, can pull you away from what's really important. When your habits and behaviors are not aligned with your Values and your Why, it has the effect of dispersing your focus and energy.

For example, the sun puts out billions of kilowatts of energy and the worst thing you can get is a sunburn. However, focus that energy and you have a laser that can cut through metal. Your Values and your Why, when combined, should act like a laser, keeping you focused on your long-term goals and on what is genuinely important to you.

Here are some examples of Why statements:
- Celebrate both our sorrows and joys together
- Be the best versions of ourselves
- Leave the world better than we found it

- Be remembered as a force for good
- Produce generations of great families
- Learn, grow and support each other's dreams
- Demonstrate unconditional love, support and growth for each other and the family
- Improve the lives of every person and animal we interact with

Your Why should be concise, inspiring, timeless, authentic and easily remembered. It serves as a filter that allows you to say no to some things and yes to others. Think about it: Every time you say yes to something, you are simultaneously saying no to something else.

Using your Why as a filter is hard. It will require you to choose between wants and needs, between 'can do' and 'should do.' In effect, between what's right for you and what's wrong for you. To do this, you'll have to be really honest with yourselves.

Imagine you're in a boat on the ocean with no map or compass. You're told to go toward that one dim light, way, way out on the far horizon. There are other lights you might see but you'll never make it to your final destination if you follow those other lights. Keep your focus on the light straight ahead and that's how you'll reach your goals.

Your Why serves as that guiding light on which you stay focused. When your Values and Why are combined, you'll discover that all your efforts become concentrated and aligned, propelling you toward your overall aligned Vision.

3. *Big Dream*[IP]

Now that you know who you are and why you exist as a couple, the next step is to determine where

you are going. The Big Dream is your long-term, larger-than-life target. It unites both of you around a common objective. In many cases, it will help you achieve things you never thought possible.

Imagine a kite without a string. It just floats aimlessly wherever the wind takes it (potentially even into the ground). Some couples are like this—they don't have a Big Dream. While they may have a rough idea, in reality, they don't truly know where they are going and certainly don't have alignment around their ideas on how to get there.

Why is the Big Dream important? As Yogi Berra said, "If you don't know where you're going, you'll end up someplace else." In other words, if you know where you want to go, agree on it and write it down, you'll have a much better chance of getting there.

It gets you asking the right questions like: What do we need to start doing differently? What do we need to change? What could we do better? By asking and answering these questions, you are starting to live by design and not by chance.

We recommend that your Big Dream have a date and is specific; these examples are all measurable in some form or fashion:

- Retire in Tuscany by 20XX
- A home that always serves as a family retreat
- Travel to all US National Parks
- Create a trust that supports 10 orphanages
- Generate $400,000 a year in mailbox money by 20XX
- Have an annual holiday with 4 generations
- Run a marathon with the entire family
- Achieve financial independence

When you share a Big Dream as a couple, you will have a guiding light by which everyone can navigate. This shared focus becomes the compass directing your energy, resources and decisions, propelling your growth forward. And that leads us to the next part of the CVP.

4. Cohesive Rituals[IP]

The next section of the CVP is Cohesive Rituals: your actions, words, gestures, customs, traditions and practices that are repeated regularly. Rituals cement your relationship

and enhance your connection. They could be things you do as often as every day, periodically, or once a year.

For instance, you might have a monthly tradition of visiting Chuck E. Cheese, or perhaps every time you're at a beach, everyone picks up a seashell. As an example, Tina and Chris have a specific place they visit every quarter to reconnect and conduct their Quarterly Sync meeting.

A Ritual could be as simple as a "Good morning babe" text when you're apart or as detailed as the 15 things you always do for the 4th of July. It could be a bedtime story or a nickname you call your daughter when you first see her after work like, "Hey, Jolly Rancher."

One of our members, Scott, picks a random state out of a jar with his family for their annual family trip. They have to research and plan it. They enjoy it. One of his favorites was Idaho which surprised him. This is an important ritual for their family and they look forward to it every year.

Interestingly, it is often the simple little things that matter the most. A friend of ours said that her dad called her 'Sunshine' every day until the day he passed. It is the small things you do often that make a huge difference.

Whichever Rituals you have, they are more than just fun things to do. They create a sense of unity. They deepen relationships. They provide comfort in times of struggle. They create memories that really do last a lifetime. They create unbreakable bonds and connections. They support your Values and your Why.

To help you get started, here are some additional examples of Rituals from a few Cohesive Couples:

- Fly fishing in Montana every spring
- Gathering at the family cottage in Michigan for the 4th of July parade
- Working out together 3 times per week
- Annual 1:1 trip with each child
- Sunday Movie Night with buttered popcorn
- Monthly sushi date night
- Annual family ski trip to Telluride
- Cooking breakfast together on Sunday mornings
- Morning coffee together before the day begins
- An evening walk to reflect on the day
- Rebuilding a car

Can you name Rituals you are already doing or would like to start?

A Ritual might even change as your seasons of life change. Kelly used to have Meat Thursdays when the kids were in football season. When the kids moved out, they continued with Meat Nights whenever the boys were back home.

These recurring actions, whether daily gestures or annual traditions, will enrich your connection and strengthen your bond even further. By adding them to your CVP, you'll be documenting them and incorporating them into your life and journey together.

> *"My partner and I have talked about our goals before, but there was no real road map. We now have that road map."*

Now that you have completed some big picture items on the CVP, it is time to get more specific in the last 4 sections: 3 Year Vision, 1 Year Goals, Rocks and 1 Commitment to Me (C2Me).

5. 3 Year Vision

The next step is to continue dreaming but focus on a more specific time-frame—3 years into the future. Creating your 3 Year Vision is like seeing the front cover of a jigsaw puzzle box; you're pictur-

3 YEAR VISION

Date: Dec 31, 20XX
Key Numbers:
- Income:
- Net Worth:
- Measurables:

ing where you want to be and what you want to accomplish in the next 3 short years.

This helps you both see and work toward exactly the same things. Using your 3 Year Vision, your combined energy will be focused on making these items happen. When you focus your joint energy, believe it or not, you will achieve most of your Vision in a much shorter time frame than you thought possible.

Again, don't get too fixated on the 'how'; we'll show you that later. Further, remember to keep dreaming—what is your ideal picture of your life in only 3 years?`

Your 3 Year Vision will have just a few numbers (e.g., net worth, financial goals) and 5-10 bullets. Those bullets should be specific enough to know if you've accomplished them and detailed enough to paint a good picture of each.

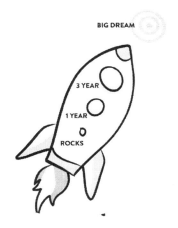

For example, 'more rental houses' is nice but not really specific. Better wording would be, '2 rental houses that are cash flow positive with a plan to get to 5.' Let's look at an example from one of our couples, Shane and Christine:

Date: Dec 31, 20XX
Key Number(s):
Income: $xxx,xxx
Net Worth: $x,xxx,xxx
Rental Income: $xx,xxx
Debt: $0

- 2 rental houses that are cash flow positive with a financial plan to get to 5
- Celebration being planned for our 20th wedding anniversary
- Accomplished 4 items from our bucket list
- Finalized drawings for our dream home
- 1 book published with 1,000 copies sold
- Focused on healthy mind, body and soul and have each reached specific fitness targets
- Have successfully executed a full family retreat each year
- Have a schedule to spend 1 month traveling each year

Your bullet points are the picture of what you see happening as you move toward accomplishing your dreams and Big Dream. Some Cohesive Couples have had fun creating a vision board as a visual image of their aligned future.

It is important to take your time and challenge each item for specificity, clarity and alignment; it is not necessary for this to be completely realistic but something like living on the moon is probably not part of your 3 Year Vision.

With that in mind, don't stress over how you can possibly achieve it. Trust the process. It works. It's fine to dream big. You'll get plenty of chances to make changes later on. By putting it on paper and staying positive, you can now move forward with a plan to make it come true.

Once your 3 Year Vision is clear and both of you agree on it, it will provide context for the next section of the CVP: 1 Year Goals.

6. 1 Year Goals

This is where we start to take your Vision down to the ground; we go from big-picture dreams to more concrete, specific steps.

Looking at the previously completed sections of the CVP, identify your numbers and financial goals for the next year. Then identify the 3–5 things that specifically need to happen in the next year to put you on a path to achieve your 3 Year Vision. In other words, what are your most important goals for the next 12 months?

Why only 3–5 goals? When you have too many goals, your energy and focus get diffused. As a result, almost nothing gets done. In our work with couples, a consistent theme is that when they take on too much, they get very little done.

Alternatively, our master couples typically have 4 or fewer goals.

Continuing with our example from earlier, Shane and Christine, here are their 1 Year Goals:

Date: Dec 31, 20XX
Key Number(s):
    Income: $xxx,xxx
    Net Worth: $x,xxx,xxx
    Rental Income: $xx,xxx
    Debt reduced by: $xx,xxx

1. Closed on 1 rental house – Christine
2. Manuscript of book sent to publisher – Shane
3. Completed a marathon – Christine
4. Free up 10 hours a week from schedule – Shane

While many of these will be shared and you must support each other and work on them together, it is important to have the 'Who will take the lead?' discussion. This helps create clarity and accountability. Take into account all the other things you have going on; this will help balance your overall load.

Assigning an 'owner' to each goal brings up another question, 'Who is best suited to do this?' Based on your personalities, interests, unique skills, natural inclinations and available time, one of you will most likely be better at leading each goal. Basically, who likes to do it and who will be best at getting it done.

Once your 1 Year Goals are clear, you'll be able to break them down even further into 90-day objectives called Rocks.

7. Rocks

The next section of the CVP is Rocks. These are your short-term objectives. They are the 3–5 most important things you must get done as a team in the next 90 days.

Why 90 days? With 1 Year Goals, everyone starts out excited and focused, but then life gets in the way. By November, very little has been accomplished— and once again, your goals have just become a nice-to-have wish list.

Rocks break 1 Year Goals down so that you are always making progress—taking little steps toward your Vision. Scientific evidence suggests that humans can only effectively focus on projects or objectives for 90 days. After 90 days, we start getting distracted. All of a sudden we're refocused on something else or nothing at all. We're letting the latest 'emergency' or 'priority' dictate where we place our energy.

Why are they called Rocks? Stephen R. Covey came up with this analogy of putting water, sand, pebbles, and rocks in a jar. Fill your jar with water (distractions), sand (minor tasks) and pebbles (important things) and you will not have room for your rocks (the most important things). However, if you start by first placing the rocks in the jar, everything else can fit around them.

Let's take a look at how Shane and Christine broke their annual goals down into Rocks:

Date: Mar 31, 20XX
Key Number(s):
      Income: $xxx,xxx
      Net Worth: $x,xxx,xxx
      Rental Income: $xx,xxx
      Debt reduced by $xx,xxx

1. Secure financing for 1 rental house – Christine
2. Complete book outline and complete draft of chapter 1 – Shane
3. Register for a full marathon – Christine
4. Hire a personal assistant – Shane
5. Schedule date nights for the quarter – Shane

As you can see, you are limiting the number to just a few (3–5) focus points; they are owned by 1 person and are very specific (you know what 'done' looks like).

In 2018, Alex Honnold and Tommy Caldwell completed the fastest ascent of the Nose route on El Capitan. They climbed this 3,000-ft vertical wall in 1 hour 58 minutes and 7 seconds, doing it in a series of 30 or so "pitches" or small steps.

These 'pitches' are like your Rocks. Small steps can take you a long way toward your ultimate goals—in a very short time. Take your 1 Year Goals and break them down into smaller, manageable chunks. Simple is better; less is more. These smaller steps are your Rocks.

You now have 4 Rock cycles to hit your 1 Year Goals and 12 Rock cycles to achieve your 3 Year Vision.

8. Commitment To Me (C2Me)

The last section of the CVP is about 1 commitment you are going to make to and for yourself, for the next 90 days. Your C2Me is in essence, a life improvement Rock.

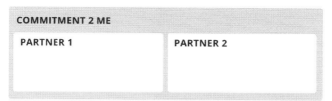

The goal is to focus on and improve one area for you, personally. If you need inspiration, we recommend using a tool called a Balance Wheel each quarter to help identify your area of focus (see Appendix A to complete your Balance Wheel). Categories to consider include:

- Relationships
- Health
- Partner
- Mindset
- Chosen Work
- Spirituality
- Wealth
- Passions

To create your C2Me, choose 1 area you would like

to work on and then, just like a Rock, write it down in specific and measurable terms.

Here are a few C2Me Examples:

- Run 3 times each week
- Host 1 neighborhood BBQ
- Do a specific Morning Routine every day
- Be (sit, walk, hike) in nature 1 hour each week
- Volunteer at church or xxx 4 hours a week.
- Have a Date Night with each child monthly

Notice these are all concrete—meaning specific and measurable – you know what done looks like. Your goal is to improve only 1 area by just a little bit every 90 days. That's your C2Me and the last section of the CVP. You'll find that small changes, over time, will have a significant impact on your life together.

So now that you know how to answer the 8 questions of the CVP, what each means and why they are all important, it is time to start.

Your CVP will be a living document—it is not irrevocable, immutable or set in stone. You don't need to have everything decided or even right. Just get started.

Here are some common pitfalls we see when couples are trying to complete their CVP and how to avoid them[IP]:

- Finish it in one sitting – Don't
- Think it has to be perfect – It doesn't
- Getting caught up in the 'how' – Trust the process
- Not being open to your partner's ideas – Be open
- Getting stuck in one section – Move on
- Thinking there is only 1 answer – There isn't

When completed, your CVP will look similar to the example on the next page. It will be your roadmap to becoming an unstoppable team.

Lockwood Cohesive Vision Plan

VALUES

LOVE, LISTEN & BE PRESENT
Love deeply and listen with empathy and understanding. Be present in all your interactions.

TAKE RESPONSIBILITY
Take responsibility of all the good and bad things. Everything is happening "for" you, not "to" you.

100 % POSSIBLE
Be abundance minded and growth oriented. If you want it, go out and get it.

HEALTHY MIND, BODY & SOUL
Take time to protect your confidence. Nourish your mind, body and soul and part of your daily life.

BIG DREAM

$X Net Worth and 100 Countries Visited as a Family

WHY

To develop deep personal connections that last generations

COHESIVE RITUALS

- Breckenridge Ski Season
- Timbuk Farms Cutting Down a X-Mas Tree
- Summer Camp
- Quarterly Family Board Meeting with Lucas & Layla
- Annual 1:1 Trip with Lucas & Layla
- Quarterly & Annual Couples Planning Meetings
- Sunday Family Day
- Consistent Mind Body & Soul Time

3 YEAR VISION

Date: Dec 31, 20XX
Key Numbers:
- Income:
- Net Worth:
- Measurables:

○ Celebration being planned for our 20th Wedding Anniversary
○ James & Lucas climbed to Everest Base Camp and have a Mission Trip planned for 2026
○ Done an amazing road trip in Norway, a sailing vacation with my parents and a trip to Japan
○ The kids love school and have found their ideal way of learning. Lucas has started a business
○ All committed to a healthy mind, body & soul and have the habits to back it up; Longevity is a focus and we are all living an active lifestyle
○ Prioritizing our Relationship & Family with regular Family Meetings, 1:1 time and Family Vacations; Kids love participating in Family Meetings
○ We have "Who's our Who's" our life
○ Our 6 rental houses are cash flow positive and we have a plan to get to 10
○ We are living in a custom built house in Willow Bend with a pool, sauna, plunge pool, games room, awesome gym and office.
○ Layla and Lucas each starting a bucket list

1 YEAR GOALS

Date: Dec 31, 20XX
Key Numbers:
- Income:
- Net Worth:
- Measurables:

⚙ Lucas & James Conquer Everest Base Camp

⚙ Contract Signed on Willow Bend House with awesome gym, games room, pool, sauna and cold plunge tub

⚙ Rebecca Co-Authors a Book

⚙ Pilot Complete for The Cohesive Couple

⚙ Financials in Place for Personal & Rentals

90 DAY ROCKS

Date: Mar 31, 20XX
Key Numbers:
- Income:
- Net Worth:
- Measurables:

⚙ Everest Training: Phase I - Once per week, treadmill for 45 minutes **(James)**

⚙ Secure Financing & Lot for Willow Bend House **(James)**

⚙ First 2 Chapters written & Chapter Outline & Roles Agreed to **(Rebecca)**

⚙ Pilot for The Cohesive Couple Built with Implementation Guide **(Rebecca)**

⚙ Selected System for Personal Financials and Data Loaded **(James)**

COMMITMENT 2 ME

PARTNER 1

REBECCA: MIND & BODY
85+ Sleep Score - 9PM in Bed

PARTNER 2

JAMES: PARTNER
6 Date Nights

Summary Of CVP

Cohesive Vision & Plan	What it defines
VALUES	Who you are and what is important to you
WHY	Your purpose together
BIG DREAM	Your long-term goal
COHESIVE RITUALS	The little and big things you do to stay connected
3 YEAR VISION	The picture of where you want to be in 3 years
1 YEAR GOALS	Your priorities for the next 12 months
ROCKS	Your priorities for the next 90 days
COMMITMENT TO ME (C2ME)	Your 1 priority for yourself for the next 90 days to improve your Balance Wheel

CHAPTER 7

We Have To Have Meetings?

WEEKLY SYNC[IP]

"It's amazing how 45 minutes a week gets us on the same page, keeps us on track, and helps us avoid miscommunication and arguments."

Wait. Really? We have to talk to each other? In a meeting? I thought this was a relationship, not a business.

In short, yes. A Weekly Sync isn't just practical, it demonstrates your commitment to continue to grow and nurture your relationship. It is how you make little steps that deepen your connection and propel you toward your goals.

Picture a couple who communicate in passing, harried by everyday life. There is always confusion about who's making dinner, which night they are going out with friends or who's doing what/when with which kid. Frustration grows. Arguments ensue over little things. Life seems really complicated.

Those dreams and goals they so intimately talked about a few years ago wither into nothingness. Deep, meaningful connection is minimal. They are both in survival mode just trying to keep the canoe afloat.

Now, imagine a couple who are making progress toward and realizing their dreams and goals. They solve issues together, even the really uncomfortable ones, and they are on the same page about who is doing what next. There are productive discussions about priorities and logistics. Schedules and activities are coordinated.

Date Nights are actually date nights—they happen because all the logistical stuff happens in the Weekly Sync. They are nurturing their relationship. The Weekly Sync keeps them sharing their life journey together, constantly growing in all areas of their lives, staying deeply connected, and maintaining an organized and manageable life—all while having fun.

Why weekly? Most human beings procrastinate by nature, waiting until the last minute to get things done. To illustrate, let's say you are planning a vacation or to buy Christmas presents. You talk about it, and let's call that point A. You need to complete all vacation preparations or Christmas shopping by a specific date, which we'll refer to as point B.

The line in the picture below represents the activity to get that stuff done. You can see the line spike just before the deadline at point B.

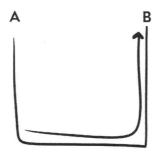

You only get that spike of activity once. If you create milestones to break it down, you create spikes of activity more often, as shown below. You get hotels booked one week and flights a few weeks later. You get 25% of your shopping done each week for a month. These little bits propel you forward toward your goals at a much faster rate.

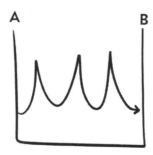

Thus the need for a Weekly Sync; it results in smaller spikes of energy, more often.

Weekly Sync[IP]

We call it the Weekly Sync because that is its intended purpose: to sync with each other. The agenda is designed to keep you connected, communicating, aligned on your goals, solving issues and taking little steps forward each week. In our experience, it is the glue that holds all the other components of the Cohesive Model together.

On the next page is the Weekly Sync agenda[IP] followed by a brief description of each agenda item.

Weekly Sync [IP]

AGENDA	APPROX. TIME
Gratitude – express what you are grateful for over the last week	4 Min
Reflections – reflect on your relationship with 4 questions	10 Min
Rocks – check in on progress	3 Min
To-Do's – check in on what's been done	3 Min
7 Day Calendar and Jobs Review – make sure the next 7 days of who's doing what are crystal clear	10 Min
Topics – anything else important on your lists	10 Min
Look Ahead – conclude with the 1 thing you're each looking forward to in the next week	5 Min

The times for each item are approximate. The key is to keep it focused and not to go down rabbit holes. Keep the objective of each section in mind. If you want to spend 15 minutes on gratitude, go ahead. Want to give it a different name? Feel free to make it your own.

You might have noted that it is about 45 minutes long. You have 10,080 minutes in a week. This is less than 0.4% of your time each week. We're only suggesting it might be worth the investment to prioritize it. Here's how each section works.

Gratitude

This is an opportunity for you to transition from whatever you were doing into a great mindset for the meeting, answering 1 question: What are you grateful for in the last week (personally, relationship, work, kids, etc.)?

Please don't skip this section of the agenda or rush through it. It plays a critical role in setting the stage for the rest of the meeting.

Reflections

This is designed to provide a deeper look into your relationship and connection. Be truly honest with your answers for the best results. It will have an amazingly positive impact long term.

Here are the questions to answer based on the last week[IP]:

1. How was my mindset?
2. How was my health?
3. How was my parenting?
4. How connected do I feel to you?

We recommend giving answers on a 1-10 scale. This will provide insight into your partner's week and will provide opportunities for you both to reflect and grow. It is a great opportunity to discuss your answers.

Great scores are just that. Low scores are just that. You'll get some of both and that is good. It helps you address issues before they become problems between you. And you will get some good tips on your partner's needs. If there is a low score, simply ask your partner, "What is one thing I can do this week to improve that score?"

Honesty is critical. If you feel disconnected from your partner, then a score of 2 or 5 is what it is. Just give a score based on your perspective and don't hold back.

It is critical that the listening partner not react to hearing low scores. Do not get defensive. Do not say bad words. This is their perspective. It is essential that the person listening has a mindset of understanding and curiosity.

Recognize that a low score is a call for action and help. Be grateful you now have the issue in the open and can address it. Again, ask your partner if there is 1 thing you can do to improve that score.
"I still remember my first '2' from Rebecca," said James. "I went from angry and defensive to checking myself and approaching it with curiosity. What

I learned and how we handled it improved our long-term connection."

This may feel dangerous and scary. It's okay—you're a normal human. When something does come up and a longer discussion is needed, don't avoid it. Use your judgment about when to address it, but don't avoid it.

This is a very powerful section of the agenda. Most of the time, you'll have great responses to these questions and it will drive a fun, productive Sync.

Rocks

You spent time agreeing on your major initiatives and goals for the quarter. Are they on track and moving forward? Do you need help or more information? Remember, Rocks are 90-day objectives that will get you to your 1 Year Goals and 3 Year Vision.

As you go through them, each person simply states in one sentence what they did last week on their Rock. Then they create a To-Do for their commitment for the next week to move their Rock forward.

For example, you might have a Rock to 'complete a budget and spending plan' or to 'finish the family trip plan for next year'. You're not giving an update on all the details; you're just staying high-level and making a weekly habit of working on it.

If there is a short discussion needed or questions, that's okay. If you feel you need a little longer, add it to the Topics section so you can dig in more. Whichever way, make this work for you. The key is to not spend 30 minutes talking about next year's vacation when that time should have been spent on calendars, jobs and other important topics.

To-Do's

This is a list of all the things you committed to doing last week during your Weekly Sync. They are 7-day action items assigned to one person and are either 'done' or 'not done.' As you go through them, short updates are okay. However, if a longer discussion is needed, put it on the Topics list—you'll get to it in a minute.

7 Day Calendar And Jobs Review

An important part of staying in sync is the review of your calendars for the next 7 days and who's doing what on the Jobs Chart (explained in the next chapter). Here, you make sure everything is agreed on and still makes sense. It is not uncommon to hear, "I thought we had a date night on Wednes-day and now you have a work dinner and I have a kid's game to go to."

> *"If you don't prioritize your life,*
> *someone else will."*
> – GREG MCKEOWN, *ESSENTIALISM*

This will keep you connected and aligned for the next 7 days. Resolve any calendar and job con-flicts for the next week in this section. Life will still throw surprises at you but at least you've managed what you can control.

Every once in a while, you'll want to expand this to look further into the future. For example, some couples review the upcoming month every 4 weeks and make sure important priorities like Date Nights are on the calendar.

At first, going over calendars and jobs can be a real slog – painful, detailed, excruciating and frustrat-ing. Relationships take work and the calendar/jobs review is work. Try to remember you're working together and are on the same team. Solve problems together, not against each other.

Topics

"It gives us a place to intentionally solve problems and once a topic goes on the list, we have to solve it. We can't brush it under the rug."

By now you've probably got a decent amount of items on your list of Topics to discuss – especially when you first start. Your goal is not to cover every item but the most important ones.

Start by identifying the top 3-5 things you need to talk about. In general, items on your list will fall into 1 of 4 categories:

1. ***Decisions:*** These are items where you need to make a decision. For example, where to go for your next Date Night.

2. ***To-Dos:*** In some cases, making a final decision might not be feasible, but determining the next

step, such as researching two potential loca-
tions for an anniversary trip, is. This becomes a
To-Do and gets assigned to one of you.

3. ***Updates:*** With these things, you're just updat-
ing each other with knowledge. This is sometimes called 'communication' or 'getting on the
same page.' An example would be, "I talked
with our accountant. Here's what she said."

4. ***Help:*** This is where you just want to talk something through or get a different perspective.
'I'm really having trouble with xxx, and I'd like
to talk it through with you' is a great example.

You'll also have other items that are called Stand-
ing Topics. These are items that you may or may
not talk about each week but want a reminder to
review from time to time. Examples could be:

    ** Monthly Calendar Look Out

    ** Next Quarter Budget

    ** Prayer/Keep in Our Thoughts List

    ** Next 3 Date Nights

**We use two stars as a reminder to keep these on the list
indefinitely.

When Topics are issues, dig deep and be curious. Try to resolve issues, or at a minimum agree on positive next steps even if it is a deep, personal issue. Further, adopt a "Progress Not Perfection" mindset and you'll have more fun.

Don't like calling them Topics? We encourage you to make this yours and make it fun. Scott and his wife met competing in Track and Field, so they call these 'High Jumps.' Another couple calls this section 'Things and Stuff.' You get the idea...

Look Ahead

With about 5 minutes left, stop and look forward. First, provide any feedback for next week's meeting such as:

- This was great
- Thanks for being patient
- We should have moved on from xxx more quickly
- I should have been more prepared
- How about we pick a place where we are less distracted?

Afterwards, pick 1 thing you're looking forward to the most in the next week. Share it. This ends the meeting on a very positive note. Further, you can both support each other to make sure it happens.

So that is how to really stay in sync amidst the chaos of everyday life. But what about handling topics, issues, problems and conflicts?

Issue And Conflict Resolution Tips

Here are 12 tips for solving issues and conflicts as a team based on ideas we've implemented from Gino Wickman's *Decide*, Dr. John Gottman's "Dreams within Conflict," and our own (personal and client) experience.

1. ***An Issue is just an Issue:*** It is just something getting in the way of the greater good.
2. ***Seek to Understand:*** Listen with an open mind and don't default to defensiveness. Another person's reality is not wrong, just different.
3. ***Fight for the 'we':*** Put egos, emotion and the past aside and focus on the vision of the big picture of your relationship. Don't let the issue come between you; look at it as something to tackle together.
4. ***Don't Ignore:*** Deal with the issues you fear most. Don't be afraid to be vulnerable. The future is brighter than the past. You can't change the past—but you can rewrite your future.
5. ***Uncover the Underlying Dream:*** Dive deeper to uncover the dreams, values and aspirations behind the issue. Share why the issue is so important to you.
6. ***Find Common Ground:*** Look for shared dreams and

common ground within the issue. Explore ways to both agree or compromise.

7. ***Brainstorm:*** Try to find potential solutions, even if they sound crazy at first.

8. ***Acknowledge:*** Be open to their perspective, even if you don't fully understand or agree. Acknowledge their feelings and opinions as valid.

9. ***Appreciate:*** Express gratitude and appreciation for their willingness to engage in the exercise and work to resolve the issue; this also applies to appreciating your differences.

10. ***Break:*** If the discussion becomes too intense or heated, take a break and come back to it when you're calmer.

11. ***Take Time***: Remember, some issues may take time and patience to resolve. Find ways to honor each other's goals and dreams within the relationship.

12. ***Disagree, Commit and Support:*** You can't always agree but you need to commit to the decision and support your partner.

And, if that is not enough, here are 4 bonus nuggets on issue processing and conflict resolution:

1. *Identify Assumptions:* Ask yourself what assumptions you are making. Think about your thinking.
2. *Be Humble:* You might not be right and certainly don't know everything.
3. *Laugh at Yourself:* Genuinely laughing at your faults, mistakes and characteristics can lighten the mood and help break through conflict.
4. *Defensiveness:* Don't Do It.

Tips For A Great Sync[IP]

Since the Weekly Sync is so important, here are some thoughts on how to have a great Sync.

- Have fun
- Be prepared
- Stay present and eliminate distractions
- This is not Date Night
  - o Date Night = fun and connection
  - o Weekly Sync = accountability, connection, celebrating progress, and working together
- Don't try to solve everything on your list in a single Sync. Prioritize.

The Weekly Sync is the foundation of The Cohesive Couple; it is the primary habit you're building that supports all the other Elements. *Please read that sentence again.*

Here's why. When life starts life'ing you, you'll already have a habit in place to talk about and solve issues together, pivot if needed and stay in sync. Further, you don't want to look up after a short 90 days or a year and say, "What just happened?" Instead you get to look back and celebrate all the incredible progress you've made as a couple.

Summary Of Weekly Sync[IP]

The Weekly Sync is the foundation and glue that holds the other Elements of the Cohesive Model together.

During this short meeting, you'll update each other on your Rocks and To-Do's. You get in sync for the next 7 days with the 7 Day Calendar & Jobs review. You'll also cover any important topics that need discussion.

Finally, you start the meeting with Gratitude and end with Looking Forward ensuring the meeting starts and ends on a positive note.

Action Tool	What It Does
WEEKLY SYNC™	The short, weekly meeting designed to keep you in sync. It is the foundation and glue that holds all other activities together
ISSUE & CONFLICT RESOLUTION TIPS	A short, compiled list of nuggets that help with conflict and issue processing

CHAPTER 8

Who's Doing What?

PINK JOBS & BLUE JOBS[IP]

"I felt like I was doing everything but so did he. We had so many stupid, unnecessary fights."

Picture a couple where roles and responsibilities are unclear. There is a lot of wasted time checking on who is doing what and when. Things get missed or done at the last minute. Life's daily tasks make life seem hectic, chaotic and overwhelming.

There are recurring arguments: who's cleaning, scheduling the kids for school, grocery shopping, preparing meals, paying bills, fixing the car, etc.?

Additionally, crucial long-term tasks like financial planning often get overlooked, and as for Date Nights, well, they just don't happen.

Both partners are putting in lots of uncoordinated effort and working hard. Both partners feel they are contributing more than the other person; both feel unappreciated for their contributions. This is a picture of a couple without a Pink Jobs & Blue Jobs[IP] chart.

This tool helps you define, clarify, and agree on who will own the various tasks of life. (Note: owning doesn't always mean doing but we'll explain this later.) It eliminates redundancies and mistakes.

It removes resentments and encourages appreciation for the other's efforts and contributions. It facilitates decision-making and problem-solving. It divides responsibilities fairly (however you decide to define that).

Pink Jobs & Blue Job's purpose is:

- To make sure the weekly and tactical things are happening
- To make sure the long-term things such as financial planning or Bucket List items are getting completed
- To minimize arguments, resentments and wasted time
- To align tasks with the person best suited to do them
- To further understand and appreciate what your partner does

"There was a lot of stuff being taken care of that I didn't know about."

Pink Jobs & Blue Jobs [IP]

When completed, your Pink Jobs & Blue Jobs chart will look like the example on the previous page. Don't like pink and blue? This works great for Rebecca and James, but use any colors you want as long as it is clear.

In addition to the Pink Jobs & Blue Jobs that are owned individually, you'll notice there are different areas for items you might want to trade off taking care of; these are scheduled on a simple calendar below the list. Once completed, you'll have complete clarity on who's doing what.

Creating this tool starts by listing all of the things that have to happen or be handled: short-term and long-term. The idea here is just to identify a short list of items that could be divided up between 2 partners. Here are some examples:

- Planning Date Nights
- Yard Work and Plants
- House Maintenance
- Auto
- Vacation Planning
- Cash, Bills and Mail
- Financial Management
- Calendar Keeper
- Holidays and Celebrations
- Meals

- Dishes
- Weekly Sync
- Pets
- Social Plans
- Garage and Attic
- Online Orders
- Groceries and Supplies
- Spirituality
- Home Projects
- Financial and Estate Planning
- Laundry
- Garbage
- Health and Doctors
- Clothes Shopping

Tired yet? Here are a few more that are specific to kids (we acknowledge the above list gets exponentially more complex with kids):

- Extracurriculars
- Morning Routine
- Bedtime Routine
- Homework and School
- Childcare

As you customize this list (and it must be customized for you), some items will be added and some deleted. The key here is that one person takes the lead on getting things done as agreed upon.

So how do you divide up the list? Some will be based on available time. Some may already be very clear. Some will seem natural. Others will be a discussion. Part of the answer should be in who likes to do it and where it naturally fits with their skill set and personality.

DNA^IP (Distinct Natural Ability^IP)

Everyone has one—a Distinct Natural Ability—some job, situation, place, or environment in which you excel. You gain energy because you are doing something you love and are great at doing it. It feeds your energy.

On the flip side, have you ever been in a role or situation where it drained your energy? Where you felt as if you were failing or letting others down? Where you felt the 'life' being sucked from your soul?

If so, you were probably not in a place where you could use your natural abilities. In short, your DNA is a collection of the things you can do best, with the most enjoyment and with the (seemingly) least amount of effort.

To help you get started identifying your DNA, we designed a tool called Gain & Drain™. It is quite simple. List all the things you do in the appropriate columns based on whether they give you energy (Gain) or deplete your energy (Drain).

Gain & Drain^{IP}

Discovering your DNA is a lifelong process but this is an excellent start. As you evaluate your Pink

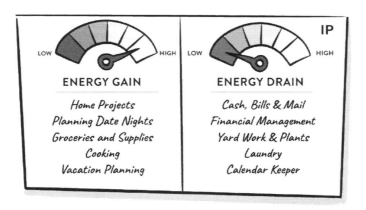

Jobs & Blue Jobs list, determine which items you can each own based on your DNA, etc. What about the remaining items?

Who's Your Who?[IP]

Now (and this has never, ever happened before in the history of life), there may be some jobs that neither of you wants to do or frankly is good at. In this case, you need to find a 'Who.'

When accomplishing tasks or achieving goals, 'Who's Your Who' can be truly transformative. If you are both disinterested, lack necessary skills, find the work abhorrent and draining, or just plain don't like to do it, you need to find someone who can and does.

If both of you hate cleaning, hiring a housekeeper not only ensures a well-maintained living space but also frees up time and energy for activities that you will find more fulfilling or important.

Similarly, for Rebecca and James, when it came to financially planning for the future (daunting for many people), the solution involved enlisting a financial advisor. Now they have a profession-

145

al Who, who can offer expertise in areas such as investing, saving for retirement or optimizing tax strategies.

As you find your Who's, someone will still need to 'own' the task. Is it a Pink Job or a Blue Job? That person is still responsible for managing your Who and making sure it gets done.

All high-performing athletes and businesses surround themselves with Who's to make them better. Why would you be any different?

With all that being said, you do have to take into account your financial situation. For example, a housekeeper or lawn care service may not be in the budget. However, simply identifying these items can help. We suggest the goal of finding the right Who's and when becomes part of your CVP in either the 1 or 3 Year sections.

Another aspect to consider is the "Who's Your Who" mindset, which prompts you to assess your goals and tasks with a perspective of collaboration and delegation, rather than relying solely on yourselves. It acknowledges that time and energy are finite resources.

It also allows you to focus on your strengths while outsourcing your weaknesses. You will not only achieve more of your objectives with increased efficiency but also strengthen your relationship by reducing stress and conflict over unwelcome tasks. To close the loop on this, we suggest you keep a list of current and future potential Who's Your Whos.

Summary Of
Pink Jobs & Blue Jobs^{IP}

Pink Jobs & Blue Jobs and the related tools will be used in your Weekly Sync and should be reviewed at each of your Quarterly Sync and Annual Sync meetings (more on this shortly) to see if anything needs to be adjusted or if it's time to find some Who's.

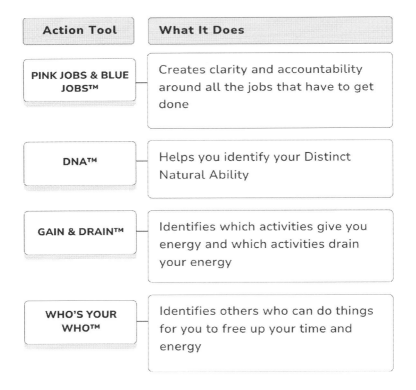

Action Tool	What It Does
PINK JOBS & BLUE JOBS™	Creates clarity and accountability around all the jobs that have to get done
DNA™	Helps you identify your Distinct Natural Ability
GAIN & DRAIN™	Identifies which activities give you energy and which activities drain your energy
WHO'S YOUR WHO™	Identifies others who can do things for you to free up your time and energy

CHAPTER 9

Money Causes Arguments?

MONEY SYNC[IP]

"When couples come together regularly to discuss their finances. They're weaving a stronger fabric of trust, partnership and shared vision for their future."

– DAVE RAMSEY, PERSONAL FINANCE EXPERT

Your monthly Money Sync is not just an opportunity to review numbers; it's a great opportunity to align on goals, celebrate progress and tackle challenges head-on. There is also an additional benefit to the Money Sync—it reduces money friction.

For many couples, money discussions are put off or only happen when there's a problem. This is understandable given that many couples are just trying to survive life and have not been given the tools or skills to talk about money. How do we know a monthly Money Sync is critical? Let's look at some facts:

- 50% of divorcees cite money as the main cause of their divorce
- 67% of married couples don't regularly discuss their financial plans or status
- 40% don't agree on how much is needed for retirement
- 66% don't have a financial plan they follow
- 30% don't even agree on their current financial status

We use a simple agenda and a few tools to make these discussions fun and productive. You'll see how this ties back to all the other Elements in The Cohesive Model.

It may seem daunting or overwhelming at first. You may say that you're not good at numbers or come up with another excuse. However, it must happen if you want to create powerful conversations that strengthen your partnership and pave the way for financial and general harmony.

Here's the monthly Money Sync agenda:

Money Sync IP

AGENDA	APPROX. TIME
Gratitude – express what you are grateful for financially	3 Min
Monthly Look Back – review the last month for lessons learned	10 Min
13-Week Cash Flow Review – review future cash in and cash out focused on the availability of funds	10 Min
Money Topics (Pick 1) – focused discussion to improving your financial understanding, process or situation	30 Min
Re-cap – review all decisions, to-do's and pick the Money Topic for the next sync	2 Min
Look Forward – share 1 lesson learned and any financial successes you are looking forward to	5 Min

Seems pretty simple, right? Now that you've seen it, let's take a short dive into each section.

Gratitude

Similar to the Weekly Sync, pick something that you are grateful for financially in the last month. It could be a big debt that was paid off, a trip you saved for, great progress on a few financial items or your job. It is a good way to start the meeting and get you in the right mindset.

Monthly Look Back

This is a short look back at the last month to compare how the month ended up against your projections (see 13 Week Cash Flow below). Here are some questions you might ask:

- Were there unexpected expenses?
- Was spending loose in some areas?
- Where could we have made better decisions?
- What lessons did we learn and how will we apply them going forward?

Our suggestion is to be realistic about lessons learned and how you will apply them going forward. It is better to make small, achievable commitments to change than promise something to each other that, in your heart, you know probably will not happen.

13 Week Cash Flow

It is not as scary as it sounds. This section of the Sync is about making sure you are investing in the future and have enough cash to get bills paid. It also helps you identify if you have extra cash so you can decide how to use it. Once you get started, it is actually fairly easy. But why would you even want to do this?

It provides you with a simple look at the next 13 weeks to identify any cash crunches. It helps you become proactive instead of reactive. It allows you to adjust spending in real-time so that you can meet overall financial goals. Finally, it helps you prepare for life's unexpected twists and turns.

Why 13 weeks? It helps look out far enough to identify any odd quarterly payments you might have to make, but it's near-term enough to be a really good reality check.

First, let's make sure we're clear on the differences between the 13 Week Cash Flow and Financial Goals.

	13 Week Cash Flow	Financial Goals
TIMELINE	Short	1+ Year
PURPOSE	Liquidity and paying bills on time	Financial discipline and limits, guiding spending, financial structure and achieving overall goals
FLEXIBILITY	More dynamic	More static
DETAIL	More detailed – tracking the exact timing of income and expenditures	More about general allocations and spending limits

The 13 Week Cash Flow is all about your available cash and how you are using it. The tool has 3 sections: Income, Investing and Living.

Here is an example:

13 Week Cash Flow

WEEK 1 BEGINS
MM/DD/YY

	WEEK 1	WEEK 2	WEEK 3	...	WEEK 12	WEEK 13	TOTAL
CASH AVAILABLE (BEGINNING OF WEEK)	0	0	0		0	0	0
INCOME							
Income 1 Deposit							
Income 2 Deposit							
Other (rental, etc.)							
TOTAL INCOME	0	0	0		0	0	0
TOTAL CASH AVAILABLE (BEFORE INVESTING & LIVING)	0	0	0		0	0	0
INVESTING							
Debt							
Big Purchases							
Investments / Retirement							
Safety Reserve							
Bucket List / Vacation							
Tax Reserve							
Other							
LIVING							
Mortgage/Rent/Car							
Utilities (Gas, Electric, HVAC, Water)							
Date Nights / Fun							
Other Autopay (Bank, not CC)							
Credit Card 1 Payment							
Credit Card 2 Payment							
Other							
TOTAL INVESTING & LIVING	0	0	0		0	0	0
CASH AVAILABLE (END OF WEEK)	0	0	0		0	0	0

For most people the first section, Income, should be fairly easy to forecast and pre-populate. For example, if you get distributions or paid twice a month, you know the weeks in which this will get deposited into your bank account.

The Investing section is about how you are using your cash to fund your financial future. It includes categories such as:

- Debt – Paying of a mortgage, car or other items to reduce debt balances
- Big Projects – Money set aside for a renovation, large purchase or other major items
- Investments/Retirement – Stocks, 401(k)s and other similar accounts that fund your future
- Safety Reserve – An emergency fund—typically 6-12 months of living expenses—for unexpected life events
- Bucket List/Vacations – Money separated to ensure you can pay for these types of expenses
- Tax Reserve – For those who have to make estimated payments or are expecting to owe taxes

You certainly don't need to allocate money to each of these categories, and you may have others that make more sense for you. This is all about funding future activities and needs. If your debt is significant, it might make sense to take care of this area first before any of the other future financial categories. So why is this before Living expenses?

Let's face it, most people spend to the level of their income. If the investment section were last, you would likely only invest what was left over after Living expenses. You would not be forced to make the hard decisions about controlling Living expenses in order to meet your longer-term financial goals.

While focusing on Living expenses first may be comforting in the short term, this mindset can lead to significant financial stress and instability in the long run. When you delay addressing financial challenges, such as not saving for retirement early or accumulating high-interest debt, you compound future problems.

On the other hand, if sacrifices are made in the short term, future opportunities and financial security are much more likely. By putting the Investment section first, it will encourage you to take a hard look at the last section, Living.

Here, you are projecting your Living expenses for the next 13 weeks. Remember, this is the cash you have available after investing in the future. You might have more categories but we tried to keep this simple. Here are the suggested categories in our tool:

- Mortgages/Rent/Car – Monthly debt payments
- Utilities – Gas, electric, HVAC, Water, Internet, TV, etc.
- Date Nights/Fun – This is a must!
- Credit Card 1 & 2 – Amount due to keep a $0.00 balance
- Other Autopay – Other automatic payments not already accounted for above
- Other – Anything else

As you do this, you can also pre-populate and re-evaluate as you get better. This is definitely a Progress Not Perfection tool. For example, you may know that utilities typically run about $500 a month and they are higher in the summer. If so, then put $600 for the summer months.

When this data is entered, you will see which weeks are tight and which have excess money. This should prompt a discussion asking:

- What do we do in the tight weeks?
- How can we adjust?
- Where can we reduce living expenses?
- Where can we invest more?
- How do we increase income?
- Are we okay on all our upcoming bills?
- Do we have any major expenses unaccounted for?

Those are just a few things that may pop up out of this tool.

We know there are some of you who will resist using this tool, others who will love it and a few who will just plain hate it. You might think it sounds difficult or complex. Let us assure you, once started and if you follow the Progress Not Perfection mindset, it will be incredibly valuable.

By reviewing a clear snapshot of what your financial situation looks like in the near future, the 13 Week Cash Flow empowers you to make informed decisions, adjust as needed, and maintain a healthy financial relationship.

Money Sync Topics[IP]

This is a chance for you to dive deep together on 1 specific financial topic. It may be retirement, kids and money, savings or many other items related to money. This is a great opportunity to get aligned with your views and actions around money.

Some Topics may need more time than allocated in the Monthly Sync. Some may be better for Quarterly or Annual Syncs. Some may not apply to you at all. In any case, pick 1 each month.

Since each of these topics will require some level of preparation, it's essential to start getting ready in advance. Here are 4 examples; a more detailed list can be found in Appendix C.

Money Sync Topic examples:
1. *Money Chart Review:* Do we have a map of all bank accounts, who has access, which are linked and the purpose each serves? Is each account's purpose clearly stated? Do we have a clear picture of what money goes in and out of each account? Does this include your investment and retirement accounts?
2. *Money Behaviors, Beliefs, and Knowledge:* Where do our money behaviors and beliefs differ? How do our different money approaches show up in our relationship? How can we further improve our financial acumen and skills?
3. *Insurance/Beneficiaries/Wills/Estate:* When was the last time we reviewed wills and beneficiaries? Are beneficiaries listed on all financial accounts? Have we assigned a power of attorney? Does someone know where to go for all death-related paperwork? Do we have the appropriate amount of life insurance?

4. **Professional Who's:** Who are our advisors: financial, investment, tax, accounting, legal, life, or personal assistant? Do we think they are doing a good job? Do we need to find replacements?

Select 1 each month, make sure to prepare and remember to have a mindset of Progress, Not Perfection—if you stick with it, you will make incredible strides. For many couples, a little additional planning, communication and alignment around money produces incredible gains.

You'll find this a great way to really sync, set and achieve goals, avoid conflict and build a stronger financial foundation that supports your dreams and strengthens your relationship.

Recap

This is a dedicated time to make sure all decisions and To-Do's are clear with responsibilities and assignments documented. This will help avoid confusion and make sure you are clearly aligned on the next steps. Also, pick the Money Topic for next month's Money Sync meeting so that any necessary pre-work can be prepared.

Look Forward

Looking ahead is a great way to end the meeting. First, review any lessons learned during the meeting and briefly discuss how you will apply those in the future. Then, identify 1 financial item you are truly looking forward to in the next month.

For example, the final payment on a specific debt, completion of a Bucket List or vacation fund, or the start of a new project. Now, you can see how the Money Sync will help to keep you both aligned and focused on your immediate and long-term financial success.

The same Weekly Sync tips apply to the monthly Money Sync. Here are a few more important thoughts:

- When you need a Who, such as your tax advisor or financial planner, schedule the sync well in advance.

You can have a separate sync with them or invite them only for that section of the sync.

- Complete pre-work before the sync. That includes having updated numbers ready and available, accounts open on a laptop, etc.
- If you don't finish a topic you can decide to go longer, wait until next month, put a critical decision on the Weekly Sync Topics list, save it for the next Quarterly Sync or Annual Sync, or put it on a list as a potential Rock next quarter.
- Keep in mind Pink Jobs & Blue Jobs when assigning To-Do's and next steps.
- If something becomes heated, take a break. Re-read the issue and conflict tips from the Weekly Sync chapter.

Additional Tools

There are 2 money items you will review quarterly and/or annually. These are:

- Net Worth
- Financial Goals

They tie back to your CVP and serve as great reviews of your overall money health.

Net Worth

This tool is typically reviewed during the Quarterly and Annual Syncs. It tells you if your Net Worth is growing or declining.

Net Worth is simply your assets (what you own) less your liabilities (what you owe). In most cases, you want to own more than you owe. For example, if you own 2 cars and a house worth $750,000 combined and owe $600,000 in total on both, your net worth would be $150,000. Here is our tool:

Family Net Worth

ASSETS		LIABILITIES	
Employer Retirement Plans	$$	Real Estate Loans	$$
Individual Retirement Accounts	$$	Personal Guarantees	$$
Bank & Other Accounts	$$	Other Debt (student, cc, etc...)	$$
College Savings Plans	$$		
Home & Personal	$$		
Business & Property	$$		
Other	$$		
TOTAL ASSETS $$$		**LIABILITIES** $$	

Net Worth
$$$

Net Worth is a key measurement of overall financial health. It's a scorecard showing you if you're moving in the overall right financial direction.

Financial Goals

This tool is typically reviewed during the Quarterly Syncs and Annual Syncs.

Each couple should have a list of Financial Goals. We suggest you find your Who for this. These should include items you put on your CVP such as:

- Income
- Cash Flow
- Debt
- Big Purchases
- Investments/Retirement
- Safety Reserve
- Bucket List/Vacation
- Savings
- Net Worth

In addition, you might create Financial Goals around kids' education, personal development, relationship development or home improvements/upgrades. Whichever Financial Goals you set, a regular update of your actual numbers against those is critical.

Disclaimer

Here is our disclaimer and it's not in fine print. We are not financial, money or investment experts, specialists, consultants or advisors of any kind. We hire our own Who's for this. We are not giving financial or money advice. We are suggesting that as a couple, you will benefit greatly from these tools and a monthly Money Sync. We encourage you to get your own Who for money and financial advice.

Summary Of Money Sync™

Given that money is a major contributor to arguments, this is a critical topic. You should hold your Money Sync monthly as well as review it at your Quarterly and Annual Syncs.

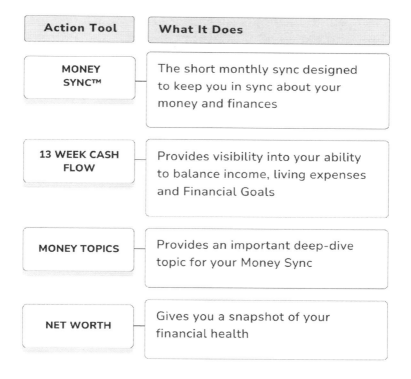

Action Tool	What It Does
MONEY SYNC™	The short monthly sync designed to keep you in sync about your money and finances
13 WEEK CASH FLOW	Provides visibility into your ability to balance income, living expenses and Financial Goals
MONEY TOPICS	Provides an important deep-dive topic for your Money Sync
NET WORTH	Gives you a snapshot of your financial health

CHAPTER 10

How Do We Keep Momentum?

QUARTERLY SYNC[IP] **AND ANNUAL SYNC**[IP]

"Our Quarterly Syncs give us the time and space to be intentional about the future together and connect at a deeper level. It is so easy to fall back into the traps of life".

Momentum is easy to lose and it is often tough to get back. Our experience (and science) shows us that 90 days is about the longest you can maintain focus before seeing unicorns and flying pigs.

In other words, after 90 days you start getting distracted, off the same page and misaligned. You lose consistency and traction. You lose sight of your long-term goals. That is why The Cohesive

Couple is not a one-time event, course or retreat; it is an ongoing journey.

Therefore, The Cohesive Journey is a proven path that includes a Quarterly Sync every 90 days.

Quarterly Sync[IP]

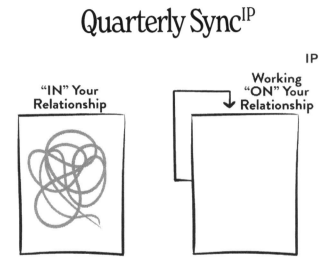

IP

"IN" Your Relationship

Working "ON" Your Relationship

Quarterly Syncs give you the space to be together to connect and align; they give you a chance to work 'on' your relationship instead of being 'in' it all the time. They give you the chance to look at your life from above and observe patterns, behaviors and recurring themes.

In your Quarterly Sync, you'll reaffirm your long-term goals and set new Rocks to ensure you're on track with your progress. You'll also take time to review your calendar for the next 3 months to align on upcoming activities. You'll have a chance to take your time on deeper issues and topics you need to talk about.

Additionally, you'll examine your financial goals to assess and make any necessary adjustments. Moreover, you'll reinforce the four Elements of the Cohesive Model while learning new tools. This is your chance to step back, take a deep breath and get back in sync.

Annual Sync[IP]

Just like the Quarterly Sync, the Annual Sync is your time to stay aligned but with your eyes not only on the next 90 days but also on the future. This is a great chance to reflect on the past year's achievements and challenges, allowing you to appreciate your journey and learn from your experiences.

In your Annual Sync, you will revisit and possibly even redefine your long-term goals to ensure they still resonate with your evolving season of life. It's an opportunity to set ambitious yet achievable goals for the year ahead. You'll create a clear roadmap for what you will accomplish.

It also allows for a comprehensive review of your financial health so you can adjust your plan for better future outcomes. You'll have the space to discuss and plan major life events, transitions, or projects that you foresee in the year ahead, ensuring that both of you are prepared and on the same page.

Moreover, the Annual Sync is an ideal time to celebrate your successes and acknowledge the effort both partners have put into achieving them. It's a moment to strengthen your bond, reflect on your growth as individuals and as a partnership, and look forward with excitement to the next chapter of your journey together.

The Annual Sync is also a great opportunity to make a trip or special occasion out of it. For example, Rebecca and James get an Airbnb every year to get away from kids, noise, and everyday life to provide themselves the time and space to reconnect and plan for the future. You could also combine this with an additional learning experience.

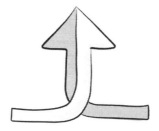

Lastly, the Annual Sync encourages you to integrate new knowledge and tools that have been acquired over the past year into your Cohesive Model. Put differently, it's about continuously refining and advancing your approaches for success. This is your moment to reset, recharge and realign, setting the foundation for another year of success.

Unfortunately, sometimes couples don't plan ahead or think they are too busy to have their Quarterly and Annual Syncs. Committing to your Quarterly and Annual Syncs is part of building a habit and holding yourselves accountable. It is part of the commitment you are making to each other.

> *"Your calendar and budget are a direct reflection of your priorities."*

Even if you've missed some Weekly Syncs or things haven't gone as well as you wanted, we can't stress enough the importance of the Quarterly Sync and Annual Sync. They are critical psychologically, emotionally and physically. And they are just a lot of fun.

Starting is easy. Staying focused and disciplined is hard work. The Action tools are designed to make life easier and simpler and keep you on track even when life starts throwing you curve balls.

Summary Of Syncs

(CHAPTERS 8 - 10)

Your Syncs™	What It Does
WEEKLY SYNC™	Keeps you in sync and is the glue that holds all other activities together
MONEY SYNC™	Keeps you in sync about your money and finances
QUARTERLY SYNC™	Celebrates progress and creates focus for the next 90 days to keep your goals on track
ANNUAL SYNC™	Takes you above your relationship to reflect, reset and strategically plan for the future

CHAPTER 11
Are You Ready?
THE COHESIVE JOURNEY^{IP}

"Every step forward in this journey is a step towards a better us."

— DAVE RAMSEY, PERSONAL FINANCE EXPERT

Congratulations! You're ready to continue your Cohesive Journey^{IP}. On this never-ending journey, you'll be working together to strengthen the 4 Elements of The Cohesive Model: Mindset, Connect, Vision, and Action.

As you work towards 100%, you'll have an increased Awareness and Curiosity about your mindset, enabling you to better handle challenges, achieve dreams, plan, build a deep, lasting relationship, laugh, celebrate and support each other no matter what.

You'll have a deep, intimate connection strengthened by a more robust understanding of each other through Kolbe A to A and Love Languages. That connection will be further enhanced through consistent Date Nights, Cohesive Rituals and other Connect tools.

By using the CVP to document your plans, dreams and goals, you'll ensure alignment. Everything from your Values and Big Dream to your 3 Year Vision to 1 Year Goals to your Rocks will be achievable.

The Weekly Sync, Pink Jobs & Blue Jobs and Money Sync tools will give you the traction and cadence you need to achieve your dreams. Problems will no longer come between you and will be easier to solve. You'll feel more in control and life will be more manageable.

You'll enjoy the Quarterly Syncs as a time to celebrate progress, connect, focus and reset for the next 90 days. You'll be deepening your connection and strengthening your relationship during your Annual Sync while reflecting, resetting and strategically planning for your future, amazed by what you have already accomplished.

The Cohesive Journey[IP]

The Big Dream

Annual Sync

Quarterly Sync

Quarterly Sync

STARTING YOUR COHESIVE JOURNEY

| Create an Aligned Vision & Plan | Begin Date Nights | Begin Weekly & Money Sync Meetings |

You will have prioritized what truly matters to you both. Together, you will be making the most of your time, talents and opportunities—realizing your full potential as individuals and as a couple. You will be acting as a team in the same canoe, moving in the same direction, in sync.

You will be saying YES to the important things for you both. You will know you have both decided to live your best life together: Aligned, Connected and Thriving.

Temperature Checks

These are 2 tools that you will use periodically to assess where you are on your Cohesive Journey. They will provide a consistent baseline to evaluate:

- How are you doing as a couple? (Relationship Check Up)
- How are you doing individually and where can you support each other? (Balance Wheel)

Relationship Check Up[IP]

Since you understand the Model and its different Elements (Mindset, Connect, Vision, Action) how about a short check up on where you are today?

Just answer the questions on the next 2 pages and total your answers for each section. Note: radical honesty will get you the best insight on where to focus your efforts.

Scale 1-5

(1-Never, 2-Rarely, 3-Sometimes, 4-Usually, 5-Always)

Relationship Check Up [IP]

CONNECTION

We check in on how connected we're feeling (actual discussions)
We have significantly more (7:1) positive than negative interactions
We strive to learn more about each other to communicate better
I know my partner's love languages and work to fulfill them
We engage in rituals (daily) and date nights (weekly)

CONNECTION   Total:

VISION

Our goals are written down and agreed upon
Our values align, and we live by them
We are aligned on our 3 Year, 1 Year and 90 Day goals
Our calendar and budget reflect our shared vision
We have quarterly and annual meetings to reset and refocus.

VISION   Total:

Relationship Check Up

ACTION

We regularly discuss progress towards our goals
We have a weekly and regular calendar review
We maximize each other's strengths and delegate all other things
We have divided responsibilities fairly and have them written down
We operate as a team to solve problems and issues

ACTION   Total:

MINDSET

I recognize that things only have the meaning I give them
I value self-development and constantly seek to grow and learn
When I make progress, I'm happy even if I don't reach my ultimate objective
I am aware and curious of my thoughts and resulting behaviour
I diligently manage my emotions through Clarity Time and healthy habits

MINDSET   Total:

185

Balance Wheel[IP]

A Balance Wheel is designed to give you a picture of your current state across 8 important aspects of your life. It will identify areas where you are fulfilled and areas that need attention. Over time, it will serve as a guide toward a more balanced and harmonious life.

Moreover, when you compare your partner's Balance Wheel with yours, you'll pinpoint areas where mutual support and assistance can be provided.

The 8 areas of your life the Balance Wheel suggests you reflect on are:
- Relationships
- Health
- Partner
- Mindset
- Chosen Work
- Spirituality
- Wealth
- Passions

As you review each area of the Balance Wheel below, use a scale of 1-10, with 1 being totally unsatisfied and 10 being completely satisfied.

Find any areas you would like to work on?

Balance Wheel [IP]

RELATIONSHIPS
- Children
- Family & Friends
- Community & Events
- Rituals   Score _____

HEALTH
- Energy
- Fitness & Performance
- Rest & Rejuvenation
- Appearance   Score _____

MINDSET
- Growth & Abundance
- Mental Health
- Growth & Learning
- Progress Not Perfection   Score _____

SPIRITUALITY
- Values & Ethics
- Relationship with Higher Power
- Connection with Self   Score _____

LIFESTYLE
- Bucket List
- Hobbies & Passions
- Fun & Celebrating
- Rituals   Score _____

WEALTH
- Income
- Assets & Savings
- Financial Freedom
- Giving Back   Score _____

CHOSEN WORK
- Purpose, Passion & Legacy
- Distinct Natural Ability
- Doing What You Love
- Filling a World Need   Score _____

PARTNER
- Connection & Intimacy
- Parenting
- Solving Problems Together
- Rituals   Score _____

APPENDIX B
Acknowledgments and Resources

First, we'd like to thank and give credit to our mentors and the thought leaders from whom we have learned so much.

Brene Brown for trust and vulnerability

Lisa Carpenter for the coaching and the two by four

Gary Chapman for love languages

Lisa Chastain for money personalities and coaching

Stephen R. Covey for abundance

Carol Dweck for growth mindset

Dr. John and Dr. Julie Gottman for the four horseman

Chad & Jenise Johnson for inspiration and the connection score

Robert T. Kiyosaki for money mindset

Kris & Reka Kluver for permission to dream

Kathy Kolbe for insights around our opposite quick starts

Lauren Lane for her incredible artistic skill

Patrick Lencioni for team health
Michelle Lichtman for the rabbit roundups
Amy McCready for mind, body and soul time
Sean O'Driscoll for Head Trash
David H. Olson for his interesting research
Suzann and James Pawelski for positive psychology
Tony Robbins for awareness and UPW
Dan Sullivan for the right mindset
Gino Wickman for simplicity and structure

We also like these resources, amongst many others:

The Seven Principles for Making Marriage Work – Dr. John Gottman
5 Love Languages – Gary Chapman
Positive Parenting Solutions – Amy McCready
Family Board Meeting – Jim Shiels
Happy Together – Suzann and James Pawelski
What the Heck is EOS? – Gino Wickman and Tom Bouwer
Girl, Get Your Shit Together – Lisa Chastain
Rich Dad, Poor Dad – Robert T. Kiyosaki
Money, Master the Game – Tony Robbins
Profit First – Mike Michalowicz
The Total Money Makeover – Dave Ramsey
Powered by Instinct – Kathy Kolbe
Who Not How – Dan Sullivan
The Gap and The Gain – Dan Sullivan

We pulled information from many sources, including the American Psychology Association, the National Foundation for Credit Counseling (NFCC), and Fidelity Investments.

We would also like to thank our Test Readers for helping to make this a significantly better book.

APPENDIX C
Money Topics^{IP}

1. ***Money Chart Review:*** Do we have a map of all bank accounts, who has access, which are linked and the purpose each serves? Is each account's purpose clearly stated? Do we have a clear picture of what money goes in and out of each account? Does this include your investment and retirement accounts?

2. ***Money and Kids:*** How are we handling money with our kids? Does our money approach need changes? Do we have agreement on boundaries and lessons we're trying to teach?

3. ***Money Behaviors, Beliefs, and Knowledge:*** Where do our money behaviors and beliefs differ? How do our different money approaches show up in our relationship? How can we further improve our financial acumen and skills?

4. ***Money Causing Friction:*** What money issues are causing problems? Is there anything about money that needs to be addressed? Have we reviewed the differences in how we individually approach money (i.e., our money approaches) and discussed them openly?

5. **Bill Audit:** Do we have a bill-paying system that's working (all bills get paid on time and checked for accuracy)? What bills have increased over the past 12 months? Are there steps, negotiations or new programs that could reduce those costs?

6. **Credit Card Audit:** Have we reviewed 3 months of credit card bills? Are there any unnecessary or unknown charges? Any things that can be canceled? Do we know the benefit programs of each and are we maximizing them?

7. **Insurance/Beneficiaries/Wills/Estate:** When was the last time we reviewed wills and beneficiaries? Are beneficiaries listed on all financial accounts? Have we assigned a power of attorney? Does someone know where to go for all death-related paperwork? Do we have the appropriate amount of life insurance?

8. **Bucket List/Vacation Planning:** What vacations are we saving for? Are we putting money aside for Bucket List items? Where and how much? Does this tie in with our 1 Year Goals and 3 Year Vision on the CVP?

9. **Fire Drill:** What happens if we lose 50% of our income? Do we have a contingency plan or at a minimum, have an agreement on decisions to be made? What happens if we suddenly get hit with a major house, car or medical expense?

10. **Safety Reserves/Minimum Account Balances:** Do we have a 3, 6 or 12-month emergency reserve? Are we

working towards one? What are the conditions under which we will use it?

11. **Holes in Our Bucket:** Where are we wasting money? What are our needs versus wants? If we had to save $5 per day, how could we do it? FYI, that's $127,000 at 5% interest after 30 years.

12. *Tax Review:* Have we scheduled an annual tax review with our tax advisor? Are our tax withholdings appropriate? Have we considered the tax implications of our estate plan? Are we taking advantage of all available tax credits? Is all our tax-related documentation organized and accessible?

13. *Investment/Retirement Review:* Where are we investing and how are we doing? Are we contributing the optimal amount to retirement accounts? Are our retirement savings on track to meet our future needs? Does our asset allocation still reflect our current stage of life and risk tolerance?

14. *Professional Who's:* Who are our advisors: financial, investment, tax, accounting, legal, life, or personal assistant? Do we think they are doing a good job? Do we need to find replacements?

15. *Donations and Charitable Contributions:* What is our giving philosophy? How much and when? To whom? What are the types of organizations we will/will not support?

Join a Community of Couples Committed to Being Their Best

Get the practical tools, support and community to strengthen all aspects of your relationship and *achieve more together* **using**

The Cohesive Couple Community

Join Today!

Are you ready to rise above the chaos of life, connect deeply with your partner, and work together to build a bigger, brighter future?

We've developed an operating system and software for you and your partner to:

A framework to create your own Cohesive Vision Plan

Weekly, quarterly and annual syncs that fosters teamwork and collaboration, making it easier to support each other in achieving dreams and aspirations

Set your goals and 90 Day Rocks together and ensure you are working toward an aligned vision of your bigger future

Establish and track to dos so you can escape the chaos and prioritize what really matters together

Find out more at cohesivecouple.com

FREE Resources
to help you on your journey:

If you're ready to dive deeper into the Cohesive Couple Operating System, you can get a sample pack of 5 of our most popular resources:

• **CVP (Cohesive Vision and Plan)** - Use this tool to align, agree and document who you are, what really matters and where you are going together

• **Weekly Sync** - A simple way for you and your partner to stay in sync and keep you work towards your aligned vision

• **Date** - Get to know your spouse again through intentional Dates using these tips

• **Bucket List** - A tool to help you identify your individual and combined dreams to experience together

• **Balance Wheel** - Use this tool to identify areas in your life where you are fulfilled and areas that might need attention

Go to cohesivecouple.com/resources

Looking for a speaker for your next event?

Keynotes, retreats, break-outs, workshops

In Person and Virtual

Rebecca Lockwood   James Lockwood   Tom Bouwer

The Cohesive Couple
as seen in
"Cracking The Rich Code"
Endorsed by
Tony Robbins